MATLAB FAST AUTOMATION

Jacob Sapir

MATLAB FAST AUTOMATION

Copyright © 2022 by Jacob Sapir

https://realtechnologytools.com

Contents

1 The Need for Full Automation

Originally, the inspiration to automate my work stemmed from wanting to get better at my craft by reducing the number of mistakes I was making. Becoming faster and doing less work were only of secondary importance.

My first epiphany was realizing that a computer doesn't forget. It makes you understand the extent to which one mistake can be leveraged to improve your craft. Every mistake becomes an opportunity to make your code more robust, resulting in an inevitable improvement in an unchanging set of tasks over time. In contrast to that, humans can inadvertently make the same mistakes even after 10 years of performing the same task. This is a non-trivial point, as it's easy to deny making mistakes on activities that are part of an already established process. These mistakes can easily be attributed to a lack of concentration, fatigue, or being overworked, thereby implying that they won't happen again and ignoring the fact that these very mistakes have been handled in the past under the same assumption of no future re-occurrence. That's why the full value of automation can seem rather abstract, considering that one of its main attributes reflects a (somewhat denied) reduction in potential problems rather than an addition of something. A subtraction is rarely seen as an improvement.

The automation of tasks resulting in higher-quality work can also be justified by the improvement in the consistency and the systematic approach with which daily activities can be carried out. Applying a procedure is a perfect example of this. Relying on your memory to make sense of the way to apply every step of a procedure might lead to errors of interpretation. Opting for the development of a script that will do that for you forces you to specify every step of the procedure; there is no room for interpretation in a script, and so it ensures a perfect replication of the results. You can then afford to pay more attention to the details knowing that you will have to do that only once.

Let's have a quick overview of where computers outperform humans, so that we can better identify where the value of automation lies. Compared to computers, humans have high variability in terms of execution time. A computer never slows down, and it never misses clicks or opens the wrong file; thus there's very little variability in the time it takes to execute a task. It also doesn't get lazy, sleepy, distracted, tired, or bored. It doesn't ask for a raise, cost money, or need vacations; it just does what it's programmed to do, 24/7, 365 days a year. It doesn't need to be in perfect conditions to be at its peak of productivity performance, and can replicate exactly the same results over an extended period of time. This book provides the tools to take full advantage of the characteristics of computers that render them superior to human beings.

2 Making Things More Practical

"General principle: the solutions (on balance) need to be simpler than the problems."

— Nassim Nicholas Taleb, *The Bed of Procrustes*

As a practitioner of MATLAB, there may be times when you're less concerned about the process of learning a skill than with the practical solution to the actual problem you're encountering at that precise moment in time. However, I'm a model-based design engineer, and I've found that using knowledge to solve an actual problem is one of the fastest ways to learn and remember something in the long run. This is why I've attempted to make everything in this book as easy to understand—and as fast to implement—as possible.

Although there is already a significant amount of documentation on the internet about MATLAB (namely the excellent MATLAB documentation from Math-Works), at times the solutions I've found from other sources seemed more complicated to apply than trying to solve problems on my own. **Someone else's solution to a problem should not take you more time to understand than solving the problem by yourself would.** Although this may seem obvious, a lot of what I've found did not seem to respect that basic principle.

Basically, I wanted this book to be a simple and fast way for you to learn how to automate everything you would want to automate. This is why I've presented numerous functions in this book, so that you can test them for yourself. This is also why I've tried to be as concise as possible in my explanations and to provide examples of how every function is used.

This book is more about the practical aspects of MATLAB and how to actually automate various tasks than it is about learning MATLAB programming in a broader sense, the reason being that a great deal of content about programming in MATLAB is readily available. What I found, however, is that there was too wide a gap between what I wanted to do and what the documentation was providing.

3 Cutting Down Your Learning Curve

Ironically, the overabundance of information about MATLAB makes the relevant information you actually need less accessible. There are an infinite number of ways to code just about anything, and you could use tons of different MATLAB commands to get to your end result. This book is not about exploring all of them, and comparing them to know which one is to be used in which situation while leaving you without a clear answer on what to do. In this book, I attempt to provide a single solution that's unequivocal and practical, not necessarily a solution that's perfect.

The logical consequence of this approach is twofold: a reduction—to a bare minimum—in the number of commands you need to use, and a reduction in the amount of time you will need to acquire this knowledge. You won't have to spend hours and hours on end to find a solution that works. Every line of code given in this book has been tested and will work on MATLAB R2013b and higher versions. You may consider this book as a basis for automating in MATLAB that you can expand upon. This is the book that I wish had existed when I started out with MATLAB.

4 Organization

Here's a quick overview of each part of this book:

- **Part I: The Basic Tools for Automation**
  This part will give you the tools to automate your tasks. After reading this, you'll know how to use matrices, lists, cells, and the basic MATLAB commands needed for automation.

- **Part II: Extract and Generate Excel Files Automatically**
  This part covers everything you need to know about automating Excel file data exportation and Excel file generation from MATLAB.

- **Part III: Manipulate Files**
  This part describes how to copy, paste, delete, and move files and folders, as well as how to automate the generation of any kind of file from MAT-LAB (illustrated with examples of Word documents, plain text, .m files, and LaTeX).

- **Part IV: User Interface**
  This part discusses the best user interfaces, depending on what you want to do and how to create the interfaces.

- **Part V: Best Practices in MATLAB: Improve Your Programming Skills**
  This final part provides a list of the best practical approaches to coding in MATLAB that I've learned and the most efficient ways to structure projects in MATLAB, and it describes how to leverage your time when writing code.

Using the Tools

Every line of code used in the book can be downloaded here:

https://github.com/jacob-sapir/matlab

Part I
The Basic Tools for Automation

This first part of the book is about the tools you need to automate in MATLAB, you can skip this part if you are already familiar with cells, matrices, and MATLAB functions such as **strtok, strsplit, numel, strcmp, str2num,** and **isempty.** Make sure to have look at the cheat sheet (second appendix) where all functions are referenced.

1 Using Cells

Cells are among the most useful structures to use in MATLAB to write data into an Excel file. Also, numerous MATLAB functions require the argument type to be "cell".

Cells are really easy to use; you just enclose within braces the name of the variable that you want to put in a cell. For example, if the variable is named "cost," then the cell is {cost}.

Command Window

```
>> cell

cell =

    cell

    '25'
```

```
1  cost = '25';
2  cell = {cost};
```

It's as simple as that. You will see in the following sections why cells are necessary for automation of Excel file generation.

2 Using Lists

Using lists is paramount, because you are going to have to use them to store the data that you want to input later on (into an Excel file, for example).

2.1 Formatting Data into a List

In order to automate something, you will eventually have to get data from other places and format them properly. In this example, we are going to take the workspace as the place that you want to get your data from.

In the following sections, I will call an array of words a "list". This is an example of a list of three cells:

```
>> list = [{'firstWordInList'}; {'secondWordInList'}; {'thirdWordInList'}]

list =

    3x1 cell array

        'firstWordInList'
        'secondWordInList'
        'thirdWordInList'
```

Let's say that you have defined a lot of different parameters in your workspace. It could be an exceedingly long list of parameters that you don't want to put into a list manually. You will often find yourself in that situation, and what you are going to want to do is combine all of these data into a list. Here's how to do that:

Command Window

```
1   variable1 = 'firstWordInList';
2   variable2 = 'secondWordInList';
3   variable3 = 'thirdWordInList';
4   variable4 = 'fourthWordInList';
5
6   % get all parameters that start with "variable"
7   list = whos('variable*');
8
9   % access the second variable in the list
10  list(2).name
11
12  % access the content of the second variable in the list
13  content = evalin('base', list(2).name)
```

```
>> formatWorkspaceToList

ans =

variable2

content =

secondWordInList
```

tools/formatWorkspaceToList.m

3 Using Matrices

This section assumes that you already have some basic knowledge about MAT-LAB matrices. If you don't, I have written an article about it. Here is the quick summary:

1. Create a matrix using the following:

   ```
   m = [1 2; 3 4]; % separate columns by a space and rows by a semi-colon
   ```

2. Get the dimensions of a matrix using:

   ```
   size(m, 1) % number of rows
   size(m, 2) % number of columns
   ```

3. MATLAB matrix: transpose, inverse and identity matrix:

   ```
   m = [1 2; 3 4];
   mTranspose = m'; % transpose matrix
   mInverse = inv(m); % inverse matrix
   identityMatrix = eye(n); % identity square matrix (nxn)
   ```

4. Extract data from a matrix:

   ```
   A = [1 2 3; 4 5 6; 7 8 9];
   C = A(:,2) % select all rows (:)  and only the second column (2)
   R = A(2, :) % select only the second row (2) and all columns (:)
   smallerMatrix = A(1:2, 1:2);
   A(2, :)=[]; % remove the second row
   A(:, 2)=[]; % remove the second column
   ```

5. Multiply a matrix: using A*B or A.*B for element-wise multiplication:

   ```
   A*B % classic matrix multiplication
   A.*B % element by element matrix multiplication
   ```

If you want more explanations, you can find the whole article here:

https://realtechnologytools.com/matlab-matrix

3.1 Define a Matrix

Sometimes you will need to organize your data in a matrix. You can do this as

Command Window

```
1   var1 = 'firstWord';
2   var2 = 'secondWord';
3   var3 = 'thirdWord';
4   var4 = 'fourthWord';
5
6   matrix = [{var1} {var2}; {var3} {var4}]
```

tools/formatWorkspaceToMatrix.m

```
>> formatWorkspaceToMatrix

matrix =

    2x2 cell array

    'firstWord'     'secondWord'
    'thirdWord'     'fourthWord'
```

3.2 Insert Rows or Columns in Matrices

If you want to manipulate matrices, you will need to know how to insert a row or a column into a matrix. In this example, we'll use the following matrix:

$$m = \begin{pmatrix} 1 & 6 & 11 & 16 \\ 2 & 7 & 12 & 17 \\ 3 & 8 & 13 & 18 \\ 4 & 9 & 14 & 19 \\ 5 & 10 & 15 & 20 \end{pmatrix}$$

This is how to do that:

Command Window

```
1   m = [(1:5)' (6:10)' (11:15)' (16:20)'];
2
3   % the apostrophe is the transpose function
4   column = (20:24)';
5   % get columns 1 and 2
6   firstPart = m(:, 1:2);
7   % get columns 3 and 4
8   secondPart = m(:, 3:4);
9
10  % insert between the second and third columns
11  m = [firstPart column secondPart]
```

tools/insertColumnToMatrix.m

```
>> m

m =

    1    6   20   11   16
    2    7   21   12   17
    3    8   22   13   18
    4    9   23   14   19
    5   10   24   15   20
```

We inserted a column in that example; however, we could just as easily have inserted a row.

3.3 Delete a Column from a Matrix

In matrices you can delete a column using brackets:

Command Window

```
>> deleteColumn

m =

    1    6   11
    2    7   12
    3    8   13
    4    9   14
    5   10   15
```

```
1   m = [(1:5)' (6:10)' (11:15)' (16:20)'];
2
3   % if we want to delete the fourth column
4   columnToRemove = 4;
5   m(:, columnToRemove) = []
```

tools/deleteColumn.m

3.4 Remove the Last or First Rows or Columns of a Matrix

You can remove the last columns by defining the matrix without selecting the last part:

Command Window

```
>> removeLastColumns

m =

    1    6
    2    7
    3    8
    4    9
    5   10
```

```
1   m = [(1:5)' (6:10)' (11:15)' (16:20)'];
2
3   % if we want to remove the last two columns
4   numberOfColumnsToRemove = 2;
5   m = m(:, 1:(end−numberOfColumnsToRemove))
```

tools/removeLastColumns.m

3.5 Reduce the Size of a Square Matrix

Using the examples above, it is straightforward to do this:

Command Window

>> reduceSizeMatrix

```
1  m = [(1:5)' (6:10)' (11:15)' (16:20)'];
2
3  % if we want to remove two rows and two columns
4  reductionNumber = 2;
5  for i = 1:reductionNumber
6      m(end, :) = [];
7      m(:, end) = [];
8  end
9  m
```

```
m =

   1   6
   2   7
   3   8
```

tools/reduceSizeMatrix.m

This is pretty much everything you need to know about matrices for automation purposes.

3.6 Access a Cell within an Array or a Matrix

Let's build on what we learned in the previous sections. In short, if you want to access a cell, all you have to do is use braces instead of parentheses. For example, if you want to access the value of a variable in a list, you will use `list(i)`, and if you want to access the value of a variable that is within a list of cells, all you have to do is use `list{i}` .

3.7 Get the Number of Cells with the MATLAB Command "numel"

Cells are also very useful when you need to know how many elements you have in a matrix or a list and that matrix or list has been formatted with cells. Indeed, quite often you are going to want to apply some kind of operation to every cell, such as adding text at the end of the content of every cell.

Here is an example of how to add the text "_TO_BE_DEFINED" to every cell:

```
1  list = [{'firstWord'}; {'secondWord'}; {'thirdWord'}];
2
3  desiredText = '_TO_BE_DEFINED';
4  % numel outputs the number of cells
5  newList = [];
6  for i = 1:numel(list)
7      newList = [newList; {[list{i} desiredText]}];
8  end
9  newList
```

tools/addTextToEachCell.m

```
>> addTextToEachCell

newList =

  3x1 cell array

    'firstWord_TO_BE_DEFINED'
    'secondWord_TO_BE_DEFINED'
    'thirdWord_TO_BE_DEFINED'
```

To do the reverse operation and remove the text we added, we need the **strtok** function. This is a useful function when needing to separate data that have a character (e.g., a letter of the alphabet or a symbol) between them.

```
1  variable = 'firstWordInList';
2  [token, remain] = strtok(variable, 'W')
```

tools/strtokTest.m

This function seperates the first argument into two parts, **token** and **remain**:

```
token =

first


remain =

WordInList
```

Then we can remove the text we added:

```
1   list = [{'firstWord_TO_BE_DEFINED'}; ...
2       {'secondWord_TO_BE_DEFINED'}; ...
3       {'thirdWord_TO_BE_DEFINED'}];
4
5   newList = [];
6   for i = 1:numel(list)
7       % every word is split in two words
8       [token, remain] = strtok(list{i}, '_');
9       % the first part is added to a new list
10      newList = [newList; {token}];
11  end
12  newList
```

```
>> removeTextFromEachCell

newList =

  3x1 cell array

    'firstWord'
    'secondWord'
    'thirdWord'
```

tools/removeTextFromEachCell.m

Another useful function to "split" strings is the **strsplit** MATLAB function. This function separates elements using more than one character. Here are 2 examples that illustrate how to use this function:

```
>> C = strsplit('test', 'es')
C =
  1x2 cell array
    't'       't'
```

```
>> C = strsplit('word_TO_BE_DEF', '_')
C =
  1x4 cell array
    'word'    'TO'    'BE'    'DEF'
```

In the next section you will understand why this is important, especially when you want to store your data.

4 Useful Functions

4.1 Compare Strings

First, you will need to compare strings to each other if you want to rewrite and modify files:

Command Window

```
>> strcmpTest

ans =

    logical

    0


ans =

    logical

    1
```

```matlab
1  text1 = 'firstWord';
2  text2 = 'secondWord';
3
4  % if text2 and text1 are not the same, the output
       is 0
5  strcmp(text1, text2)
6
7  % give the value "firstWord" to the variable text2
8  text2 = text1;
9
10 % if text2 and text1 are the same, the output is 1
11 strcmp(text1, text2)
```

tools/strcmpTest.m

4.2 Convert Data

When reading and writing data into files, you will probably need to convert numbers to string values or vice versa. This can be done as follows:

```
1  % num2str convert a number to a string
2  numberToConvertToStr = 1;
3  stringValue = num2str(numberToConvertToStr);
4
5  % str2num convert a string to a number
6  stringToConvertToNb = '3';
7  numberValue = str2num(stringToConvertToNb);
8
9  % you can check the type using the function class
10 class(numberValue) % (double is a type of number)
11 class(stringValue) % (char is a type of string)
```

```
>> conversionStringNumber

ans =

double

ans =

char
```

tools/conversionStringNumber.m

4.3 Ensure Content

In some situations, you will need to make sure that a data file you have is not empty (for example, when writing data to an excel file; see chapter II). To do this, you can use the **isempty** function:

```
>> isemptyTest
```

```
1  % if we define an empty variable, isempty outputs 1
2  variable = [];
3  isempty(variable)
4
5  % otherwise, isempty outputs 0
6  variable = 1;
7  isempty(variable)
```

```
ans =

  logical

  1

ans =

  logical

  0
```

tools/isemptyTest.m

5 A Very Useful Function

In this section, I will present a very versatile function that I defined myself and that I personally use very often.

Basically, this function illustrates the use of lists and cells in a way that is very useful. This function is going to take two lists as inputs, and it is going to output the differences between those lists. One output will be the elements that are in the first list but not in the second list, and the other output will be the elements that are in the second list but not in the first list.

In what context can you use this function? You can use it when you need to compare the elements that are in an earlier version of a list to those in a newer version of it. For example, if you have two documents and one is older than the other, you may want to see the differences between the two. Using the old document information as one list and using information on the new document as another list, you can determine what has been added to this document and what has been removed from it. Here is the function that can perform that operation:

```matlab
function [newElements removedElements] = newOld(oldList, newList)

% check that no name occurs twice in the old and new lists
checkElementRedundancy(oldList);
checkElementRedundancy(newList);
referenceList = oldList; % look for elements added to the new list relative to the old one
newElements = getAddedElements(referenceList, newList);
referenceList = newList; % look for elements added to the old list relative to the new one
removedElements = getAddedElements(referenceList, oldList);

end

function addedElements = getAddedElements(referenceList, list)

addedElements = [];
for i = 1:numel(list)
    notAdded = 0;
    elementCandidate = list(i);
    for j = 1:numel(referenceList)
        elementReferenceList = referenceList(j);
        if strcmp(elementCandidate, elementReferenceList)
            notAdded = 1; % if an element in is found in the reference list, it is not new
            break
        end
    end
    if ~notAdded
        addedElements = [addedElements; elementCandidate];
    end
end

end

function checkElementRedundancy(list)

for i = 1:numel(list)
    nameLoop1 = list(i);
    for j = (i+1):numel(list)
        nameLoop2 = list(j);
        notARedundancy = ~strcmp(nameLoop1, nameLoop2);
        assert(notARedundancy, 'The same name occurs twice in a list');
    end
end

end
```

tools/newOld.m

Be careful, when using this function. You must use lists of **cells**; otherwise it won't work. I will not detail how this function was implemented because the goal here is merely to know how to use it. This is an example of how you can use this function:

```
1  listOfVarOldModel = [{'weight'}; {'speed'}; {'size'}; {'yaw'}; {'pitch'}; {'roll'}; ...
2      {'width'}; {'wheelTorque'}; {'thrust'}; {'acceleration'}; {'lateralPosition'}; ...
3      {'horizontalPosition'}; {'longitudinalPosition'}];
4
5  listOfVarNewModel = [{'x'}; {'weight'}; {'speed'}; {'y'}; {'size'}; {'yaw'}; {'pitch'}; ...
6      {'roll'}; {'width'}; {'wheelTorque'}; {'thrust'}; {'acceleration'}; {'z'}];
7
8  [newElements removedElements] = newOld(listOfVarOldModel, listOfVarNewModel)
```

tools/compareLists.m

This example illustrates that even with a list of thirteen elements, it is not easy to understand what happened at first glance. But by using this function, it becomes apparent that the elements "longitudinalPosition," "lateralPosition," and "horizontalPosition" have been renamed in "x," "y," and "z," respectively:

```
>> compareLists

newElements =

  3x1 cell array

    'x'

    'y'

    'z'

removedElements =

  3x1 cell array

    'lateralPosition'

    'horizontalPosition'

    'longitudinalPosition'
```

Now imagine that you have hundreds of variables, so that knowing the differences between two versions suddenly goes from being a time-consuming task to one that would be prohibitive in the absence of a tool such as this function.

For the sake of the example, the lists have been defined manually. Obviously, if you had to define these lists in a real-life example, it would be difficult to do so using this function. In the next chapter, you will learn how to extract those lists automatically from an Excel file.

Challenges:

1. Find an instance in your day-to-day workflow where comparing lists of elements could be helpful, provided that you know how to extract the lists from the files in which they're located.

2. Use the script *compareLists.m* by manually inserting the lists of elements you identified. You will be able to improve this script in the next chapter by defining those lists automatically.

3. Have a look at the first appendix and see if you can start automating your work. This is a challenge because a lot of concepts from this appendix have not been explained yet.

6 Key Takeways

(1) Use **cells** to separate elements in a list or a matrix.

(2) Use **numel** to count the number of elements in a list.

(3) Use **strtock** and **strsplit** to separate words according to a specific rule.

(4) Use **strcmp** to compare words or texts.

(5) Use **num2str** and **str2num** to convert data.

(6) Use **isempty** to ensure that a variable contains something.

(7) Use the function **newOld** to compare lists.

Part II
Extract and Generate Excel Files Automatically

The reason why it is crucial to know how to generate and manipulate Excel files is that Excel is one of the most powerful tools for storage, manipulation, and filtering of data. First, it is used in almost every single professional environment. Why should you care? Because if you want to work with other people on a project, you are going to have to use common tools to store data you want to share. For example, if you are working on a Simulink model from which code is going to be generated, useful data to share could be the parameters you are using in your model, the data type of these parameters, the number of parameters, etc.

Such information can give you an idea of the amount of computer memory needed to implement your model. It can also be very useful to have the names and values of the parameters of your model in a single document, in case you want to adjust some of the parameters, for example. Such a document can then be archived so that you have a snapshot of your model at a particular instant in time. The performance of this configuration is then saved as a backup in case of potential future accidental deterioration of your model.

Secondly, Excel is an all-around tool and can be used in a variety of situations that are not necessarily related to Simulink. Excel has become one of the mandatory tools in industry today. For example, most of the extractions of data from a database are made in Excel format. In that context, MATLAB is an excellent tool both for processing these data and for generating documentation of them.

Another example would be when the requirements of a Simulink model are extracted from a database in Excel format. The requirements of your model are obviously evolving, and new Excel files that satisfy the updated requirements can be delivered on a regular basis. If that is the case, having a way to extract only the requirements that have changed can be a powerful time saver, especially as the number of requirements tends to grow over time.

1 Read an Excel File

1.1 Xlsread Basic Syntax

Here's the basic syntax to import data from Excel into MATLAB:

```
[numbers, txt, txtAndNumbers] = xlsread(excelFileName);
```

1. `numbers`: numbers contained in your Excel file.

2. `txt`: text contained in your Excel file.

3. `txtAndNumbers`: text and numbers contained in your Excel file.

1.2 Xlsread MATLAB Example

As we've seen in the previous chapter, knowing how to extract content from an Excel File is essential if you want to automate the analysis of the data. Let's see the standard and easiest way to read an Excel file.

First, let's look at some details about how this works through an actual example. Let's say I have the following Excel file named "excelFile.xlsx:"

	A	B	C
1	firstRowWithContent		
2	otherCell		
3		3	
4	otherCell		
5		5	
6		6	
7	otherCell		
8		7	
9	otherCell		
10			
11			

Then, applying the previous basic syntax to read it, we get:

```
1  excelFileName = 'excelFile.xlsx'; % name of the file
2  [numbers, txt, txtAndNumbers] = xlsread(excelFileName);
```

So, let's examine the outputs of the **xlsread** MATLAB command:

```
>> numbers          >> txt                      >> txtAndNumbers

numbers =           txt =                       txtAndNumbers =

        3           9x1 cell array              9x1 cell array
      NaN
        5             'firstRowWithContent'       'firstRowWithContent'
        6             'otherCell'                 'otherCell'
      NaN             ''                          [            3]
        7             'otherCell'                 'otherCell'
                      ''                          [            5]
                      ''                          [            6]
                      'otherCell'                 'otherCell'
                      ''                          [            7]
                      'otherCell'                 'otherCell'
```

As you can see, the three outputs are not of the same data type:

- numbers is an **array**: this means that you can access the content of an element using parentheses: numbers(i)

- text is a **cell array**: this means that you can access the content of a cell using braces: text{i}

- numbersAndText is a **cell array**: this means that you can access the content of a cell using braces: numbersAndText{i}

Now that we've seen how to extract different data types, we will focus on extracting text for the rest this chapter. Subsquently, we will use the Excel file *excelTestFile.xlsx* as an example:

	A	B	C	D	E
1	Title Column 1	Title Column 2	Title Column 3	Title Column 4	Title Column 5
2	row 1 column 1	row 1 column 2	row 1 column 3	row 1 column 4	row 1 column 5
3	row 2 column 1	row 2 column 2	row 2 column 3	row 2 column 4	row 2 column 5
4	row 3 column 1	row 3 column 2	row 3 column 3	row 3 column 4	row 3 column 5
5	row 4 column 1	row 4 column 2	row 4 column 3	row 4 column 4	row 4 column 5

1.3 Standard Extract

An Excel file can have more than one sheet, so you need to specify the one you want to extract. Here are the two ways to specify the sheet to read using the **xlsread** MATLAB command:

1. Using the number of the sheet

```
1  sheetNumber = 1;
2  flNm  = 'excelTestFile.xlsx';
3  [~, txt, ~] = xlsread(flNm, sheetNumber);
```

2. Using the name of the sheet

```
1  sheetName = 'Sheet1';
2  flNm  = 'excelTestFile.xlsx';
3  [~, txt, ~] = xlsread(flNm, sheetName);
```

If you're not concerned about selecting any data in particular (you just want to extract all the data on that sheet), then extracting a specific sheet is straightforward, for example you can use the following:

```
1  sheetNumber = 1;
2  fileName = 'excelTestFile.xlsx';
3  [~, txt, ~] = xlsread(fileName, sheetNumber);
4  txt
```

excel/standardExcelExtract.m

We get

```
>> standardExcelExtract

txt =

  5×5 cell array

  Columns 1 through 4

    'Title Column 1'   'Title Column 2'   'Title Column 3'   'Title Column 4'
    'row 1 column 1'   'row 1 column 2'   'row 1 column 3'   'row 1 column 4'
    'row 2 column 1'   'row 2 column 2'   'row 2 column 3'   'row 2 column 4'
    'row 3 column 1'   'row 3 column 2'   'row 3 column 3'   'row 3 column 4'
    'row 4 column 1'   'row 4 column 2'   'row 4 column 3'   'row 4 column 4'

  Column 5

    'Title Column 5'
    'row 1 column 5'
    'row 2 column 5'
    'row 3 column 5'
    'row 4 column 5'
```

1.4 Narrow Down and Select the Data to Be Extracted

If you want to extract the data in a particular section of this sheet, you can use a follow-up argument in the function:

```
1  fileName = 'excelTestFile.xlsx';
2  sheetNumber = 1;
3  firstSelectedRow = '1';
4  lastSelectedRow = '4';
5  firstSelectedColumn = 'A';
6  lastSelectedColumn = 'B';
7  cellRange = [firstSelectedColumn firstSelectedRow ':' lastSelectedColumn lastSelectedRow];
8  [~, txt, ~] = xlsread(fileName, sheetNumber, cellRange);
```

excel/cellRangeExample.m

However, I would advise against this method. "But what if I don't need all the data," you ask, then remove the data you don't want after the extraction. The reason why I promote this method of extraction is that it's easier to manipulate numbers than letters in the cell range selection when you're using it from the xlsread MATLAB function. If you are using letters, you will have to answer questions such as "How do I increment a letter automatically"?, which is not easy to answer.

Let's say you want to get the first column of an Excel file. This is the way I do it:

```
1  function firstColumn = getFirstExcelColumn(filename, sheetNumber)
2
3  % get the data in the Excel file
4  [~, txt, ~] = xlsread(filename, sheetNumber);
5
6  % get all the data stored in the first column
7  columnNumber = 1;
8  firstColumn = txt(1:end, columnNumber); % 1:end = select rows from the 1st to the last
9
10 end
```

excel/getFirstExcelColumn.m

Using the following test environment, we get:

```
>> testEnvironmentFirstColumn

firstColumn =

  5x1 cell array

    'Title Column 1'
    'row 1 column 1'
    'row 2 column 1'
    'row 3 column 1'
    'row 4 column 1'
```

```
1  flNm = 'excelTestFile.xlsx';
2  sheetNb = 1;
3  firstColumn = getFirstExcelColumn(flNm, sheetNb)
```

excel/testEnvironmentFirstColumn.m

As you can see here, the information extracted is a list of cells (notice the pair of quotation marks enclosing each item). This explains the need for cells when manipulating Excel files: this is how it's done in MATLAB by default. This is not the only reason for doing it this way as we will see in the following sections.

1.5   Extract a Selection of Columns

In this section, I will show you how you can extract a selection of columns (you could also extract a selection of rows by using those tools).

```
1  function columnSelected = getSelectedColumns(filename, sheetNumber, columnSelection)
2
3  % get the data in the Excel file
4  [~, txt, ~] = xlsread(filename, sheetNumber);
5
6  % get and format as a matrix of all the desired columns from the column selection
7  columnSelected = [];
8  for i = 1:numel(columnSelection)
9      currentColumn = txt(1:end, columnSelection{i});
10     columnSelected = [columnSelected currentColumn];
11 end
12
13 end
```

excel/getSelectedColumns.m

Here is the test environment to test this function:

```
1  filename = 'excelTestFile.xlsx';
2  sheetNumber = 1;
3  columnSelection = [{1} {3} {5}];
4  columnSelected = getSelectedColumns(filename, sheetNumber, columnSelection)
```

excel/testEnvironmentSelectedColumns.m

Here are the results of using this function:

```
>> testEnvironmentSelectedColumns

columnSelected =

  5×3 cell array

    'Title Column 1'    'Title Column 3'    'Title Column 5'
    'row 1 column 1'    'row 1 column 3'    'row 1 column 5'
    'row 2 column 1'    'row 2 column 3'    'row 2 column 5'
    'row 3 column 1'    'row 3 column 3'    'row 3 column 5'
    'row 4 column 1'    'row 4 column 3'    'row 4 column 5'
```

This is everything you need to know about extracting information from an Excel file. Obviously, there are a lot of other things that could come in handy in specific situations; however, this book is about cutting your learning curve by showing what works in 99% of the cases that you will encounter. The remaining 1% would take pages and pages of information to explain. It wouldn't be worth your time (or mine) to explain all of that here.

2 Automation of Excel File Generation

If you need to document something using an Excel file, you may want to automate the generation of that file. You'll learn how to do this in the section that follows.

2.1 Standard Generation

Similar to the **xlsread** MATLAB function, the function to use in writing to an Excel file is the following:

```
1   % first we define what to write
2   variable1 = 'firstWordInList';
3   variable2 = 'secondWordInList';
4   variable3 = 'thirdWordInList';
5   variable4 = 'fourthWordInList';
6   matrix = [{variable1} {variable2}; {variable3} {variable4}];
7
8   % then we write it
9   fileName = 'excelTestWritingFile.xlsx';  % name of the file
10  sheetNumber = 1;                         % number of the sheet to write to
11  data = matrix;                           % data defined as a matrix
12  xlswrite(fileName, data, sheetNumber);   % write the data
```

excel/standardExcelWriting.m

This function will basically write data to an Excel file if the file exists. If it doesn't, the Excel file will be generated. For this function it will be helpful to indicate the cell range. However, I will show you later how to bypass the need to indicate the letters in the cell range.

2.2 How to Store a Column in an Excel File

First, you have to be careful not to write empty data to your Excel file; otherwise, there will be an error. The following function stores a list of elements in the first column of the first sheet of an Excel file:

```
1  function storeColumn(filename, data, sheetNumber)
2
3  % prevent errors in case of empty data
4  if isempty(data)
5      data = {''};
6  end
7
8  % select the cell range in which to store the data
9  firstRow = 1;
10 lastRow = size(data, 1);
11 cellRange = ['A' num2str(firstRow) ':A' num2str(lastRow)];
12
13 % store the column in the Excel file
14 xlswrite(filename, data, sheetNumber, cellRange);
15
16 end
```

excel/storeColumn.m

You can then test this environment by using the following script:

Content of excelTestWritingFile.xlsx

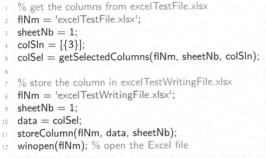

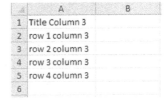

```
1  % get the columns from excelTestFile.xlsx
2  flNm = 'excelTestFile.xlsx';
3  sheetNb = 1;
4  colSln = [{3}];
5  colSel = getSelectedColumns(flNm, sheetNb, colSln);
6
7  % store the column in excelTestWritingFile.xlsx
8  flNm = 'excelTestWritingFile.xlsx';
9  sheetNb = 1;
10 data = colSel;
11 storeColumn(flNm, data, sheetNb);
12 winopen(flNm); % open the Excel file
```

excel/testEnvironmentStoreColumns.m

This script extracts the data from the existing Excel file and writes it to the new Excel file that was generated by use of this function. In this example the third column was extracted from the existing file and stored in the first column of the new Excel file.

2.3   How to Store a Matrix in an Excel File

In this section you will see how to store information in an Excel file using a matrix. As we've seen previously, the cell ranges need to be input to the function just described. The problem is that since you need letters, it becomes difficult to automatically convert the size of the matrix you want to the actual letters that are needed in the argument of this function. Here is how to do that:

```
function storeMatrix(matrix, fileName, sheetNumber, sheetName, fullPath, offset)

versionNumber = 'v2.0';
disp(['Current version: ' versionNumber]);

if isempty(matrix)
    matrix = {''};
end

if nargin < 6
    offset.row = 0;
    offset.column = 0;
end

if nargin < 5
    fullPath = pwd;
end

if nargin < 4
    sheetName = '';
end

if nargin < 3
    sheetNumber = 1;
end

currentDir = pwd;
cd(fullPath);

% add the row and column offset to the range
cellRange = computeCellRange(matrix, offset);

% write down the data
xlswrite(fileName, matrix, sheetNumber, cellRange);

% rename the sheet if sheetName is not empty
renameXlsxSheet(fileName, sheetNumber, sheetName, fullPath);

cd(currentDir);

end

function cellRange = computeCellRange(matrix, offset)

firstRow = 1 + offset.row;
lastRow = size(matrix, 1) + firstRow - 1;
```

```
47  firstCol = dec2base27(1 + offset.column);
48  lastCol = dec2base27(base27dec(firstCol) + size(matrix, 2) − 1);
49  cellRange = [firstCol num2str(firstRow) ':' lastCol num2str(lastRow)];
50
51  end
52
53  function string = index_to_string(index, first_in_range, digits)
54
55  letters = 'A':'Z';
56  working_index = index − first_in_range;
57  outputs = cell(1,digits);
58  [outputs{1:digits}] = ind2sub(repmat(26,1,digits), working_index);
59  string = fliplr(letters([outputs{:}]));
60
61  end
62
63  function s = dec2base27(d)
64  %   DEC2BASE27(D) returns the representation of D as a string in base 27,
65  %   expressed as 'A'..'Z', 'AA','AB'...'AZ', and so on. Note, there is no zero
66  %   digit, so strictly we have hybrid base26, base27 number system. D must be a
67  %   negative integer bigger than 0 and smaller than 2^52.
68  %
69  %   Examples
70  %       dec2base(1) returns 'A'
71  %       dec2base(26) returns 'Z'
72  %       dec2base(27) returns 'AA'
73  %   --------------------------------------------------
74
75  d = d(:);
76  if d ~= floor(d) || any(d(:) < 0) || any(d(:) > 1/eps)
77      error(message('MATLAB:xlswrite:Dec2BaseInput'));
78  end
79  [num_digits, begin] = calculate_range(d);
80  s = index_to_string(d, begin, num_digits);
81
82  end
83
84  function d = base27dec(s)
85  %   BASE27DEC(S) returns the decimal of string S which represents a number in
86  %   base 27, expressed as 'A'..'Z', 'AA','AB'...'AZ', and so on. Note, there is
87  %   no zero so strictly we have hybrid base26, base27 number system.
88  %
89  %   Examples
90  %       base27dec('A') returns 1
91  %       base27dec('Z') returns 26
92  %       base27dec('IV') returns 256
93  %   --------------------------------------------------
94
95  if length(s) == 1
96      d = s(1) −'A' + 1;
```

```matlab
 97    else
 98        cumulative = 0;
 99        for i = 1:numel(s)-1
100            cumulative = cumulative + 26.^i;
101        end
102        indexes_fliped = 1 + s - 'A';
103        indexes = fliplr(indexes_fliped);
104        indexes_in_cells = mat2cell(indexes, 1, ones(1,numel(indexes))); %#ok<MMTC>
105        d = cumulative + sub2ind(repmat(26, 1,numel(s)), indexes_in_cells{:});
106    end
107
108 end
109
110 function [digits, first_in_range] = calculate_range(num_to_convert)
111
112 digits = 1;
113 first_in_range = 0;
114 current_sum = 26;
115 while num_to_convert > current_sum
116     digits = digits + 1;
117     first_in_range = current_sum;
118     current_sum = first_in_range + 26.^digits;
119 end
120
121 end
122
123 function renameXlsxSheet(fileName, sheetNumber, sheetName, fullPath)
124
125 if ~isempty(sheetName)
126     % 1. open Activex server
127     excelPath = fullfile(fullPath, fileName);
128     excel = actxserver('Excel.Application');
129     document = excel.Workbooks.Open(excelPath);
130
131     % 2. process the file
132     document.Worksheets.Item(sheetNumber).Name = sheetName;
133     document.Save % # save to the same file
134
135     % 3. close excel
136     document.Close(false); % close the document
137     excel.Quit; % close excel
138     delete(excel); % delete server object
139 end
140
141 end
```

excel/storeMatrix.m

As I said, this is a bit tricky to do and you don't need to understand the code to make it work. A part of this code is actually taken from the **xlswrite** MATLAB function. I don't fully understand it myself but I do understand how to use it. All you need to know is that some of these functions are used to convert numbers into letters and letters into numbers.

This is an example of extracting the columns 1 and 3 from the file *excelTestFile.xlsx* and generating a file called *excelMatrixFile* with the content extracted from the *excelTestFile.xlsx* written and shifted five columns to the right and three rows from the top:

```
1   % get the columns from the excel file excelTestFile.xlsx
2   filename = 'excelTestFile.xlsx';
3   sheetNumber = 1;
4   columnSelection = [{1} {3}];
5   columnSelected = getSelectedColumns(filename, sheetNumber, columnSelection);
6
7   filename = 'excelMatrixFile.xlsx';
8   sheetNumber = 1;
9   data = columnSelected;
10  % fullPath is the location of the Excel file
11  fullPath = pwd; % pwd is the path to the current folder
12  % start writing on the row rowOffset+1 (offset.row = 0 => first row of the Excel File)
13  offset.row = 3;
14  % start writing on the column columnOffset+1 (offset.column = 0 => first column)
15  offset.column = 5;
16  % sheetName is the name of the sheet you want to give
17  sheetName = '';
18  storeMatrix(data, filename, sheetNumber, sheetName, fullPath, offset);
19  winopen(filename)
```

excel/storeMatrixTestEnvironment.m

We get:

◢	A	B	C	D	E	F	G
1							
2							
3							
4						Title Column 1	Title Column 3
5						row 1 column 1	row 1 column 3
6						row 2 column 1	row 2 column 3
7						row 3 column 1	row 3 column 3
8						row 4 column 1	row 4 column 3

3 Key Takeaways

(1) To extract content from an Excel file use the **xlsread** MATLAB function and remove the useless content from the extract.

(2) Use the syntax `xlsread(fileName, sheetNumber)` and `xlsread(fileName, sheetName)` to specify the sheet you want to extract.

(3) To generate an Excel file use either the **xlswrite** MATLAB function if you only want to write the data into the Excel file or use **storeMatrix** if you need to write the content at a precise location.

Part III
Manipulate Files

1 Move, Copy, Rename, Create, and Remove Folders and Files

To keep yourself organized and avoid having tons of files in your current folder, you may want to move, copy, rename or remove folders and files that you created.

1.1 Move a File

If you want to move a file, you can do so as follows:

```
1  fileName = 'excelTestFile.xlsx';
2  destination = fullfile(pwd, 'newFolder'); % pwd is the current folder location
3  movefile(fileName, fullfile(destination, fileName));
```

fileMan/moveAFile.m

The destination is the location to which you want to move your file. The **fullfile** MATLAB function is a simple way to create a path depending on the operating system you are using:

On Windows	*On Linux*
`>> fullfile('my', 'path')`	`>> fullfile('my', 'path')`
`ans =`	`ans =`
`my\path`	`my/path`

If you know you will only use Windows, using a "\" will work to create a path instead of using **fullfile**, but I do recommend using the **fullfile** function in general.

1.2 Rename a File

Renaming a file consists of keeping it at its existing location but with a different name:

```
1  fileName = 'excelTestFile.xlsx';
2  newFileName = 'newExcelName.xlsx';
3  % keep the file at its existing location but with a different name
```

```
4  movefile(fileName, newFileName);
```

fileMan/renameAFile.m

1.3 Copy a File

When you want to modify a file but you want to make sure you are not going to
damage the original file, you may want to make a copy of the original file. Here is
how to do that:

```
1  fileToCopy = 'newExcelName.xlsx';
2  destination = fullfile(pwd, '..');          % .. is the folder up one level
3  copyfile(fileToCopy, fullfile(destination, fileToCopy))
```

fileMan/copyAFile.m

1.4 Create a Folder

To stay organized, you may want to create folders and move the documents you
generate to a single new folder. This is required when you generate files with the
same name at a fixed location. If you don't create a separate folder for each copy of
a file, the generation will be erroneous because of the name redundancy. You can
create a folder using the **mkdir** command:

```
1  folderName = 'newFolder';
2  mkdir(folderName);
```

fileMan/createAFolder.m

1.5 Move or Delete a Folder

You can also delete a folder using the **rmdir** command:

```
1  folderName = 'newFolder';
2  rmdir(folderName, 's')  % 's' is necessary when folderName is not empty
```

fileMan/deleteAFolder.m

Or just move the folder using the **movefile** command:

```
1  folderName = 'newFolder';
2  destination = fullfile(pwd, '..');
3  movefile(folderName, fullfile(destination, folderName));
```

fileMan/moveAFolder.m

1.6   Use the Clock

There are 2 main reasons to use the **clock** command:

1. When you manipulate files and folders automatically it is nice to know what your code did (e.g., what is the last file or folder you've created).

2. When you genereate files and folders in the same location, you need them to have different names because you can't have the same name twice in a folder.

To help with these issues you can generate names based on the current time using the **clock** command. Here's an example of using the clock to generate a file or folder name on May 4, 2002 at 9:05 am:

Command Window

```
1  c = clock;
2  y = num2str(c(1)); % year
3  m = num2str(c(2)); % month
4  d = num2str(c(3)); % day
5  h = num2str(c(4)); % hour
6  m = num2str(c(5)); % minute
7  flNm = ['report_' m '.' d '.' y '@' h 'h' m 'm']
```

```
>> useTheClock

flNm =

report_5.4.2002@9h05m
```

fileMan/useTheClock.m

1.7 Read All Files in a Folder

Using the **dir** MATLAB command as the following, you will have seven folders and files in total:

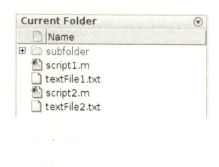

Command Window

```
>> filesAndFolders = dir

filesAndFolders =

    7x1 struct array with fields

        name
        folder
        date
        bytes
        isdir
        datenum
```

In addition to these 5 files and folders, MATLAB always considers:

- the current folder: "."

- the "up a level" folder: ".."

By specifying the extension of files you want listed, you then don't have the 2 additional folders. Moreover, if you want to see in the current folder and its subfolders, you can use '**':

Specify an Extension

```
>> mFl = dir('*.m')

mFl =

    2x1 struct array with fields

        name
        folder
        date
        bytes
        isdir
        datenum
```

See Folder and Subfolders

```
>> txtFl = dir(fullfile('**', '*.txt'))

txtFl =

    3x1 struct array with fields

        name
        folder
        date
        bytes
        isdir
        datenum
```

As you can see there is a file called "textFile3.txt" in the folder called subfolder, that's why there is 3 elements in the txtFl structure array:

Command Window

```
>> txtFl(3).name

ans =

textFile3.txt
```

If you want to list all files independent of their extension, you can do so using the "isdir" field of the filesAndFolders structure array. Its value is a boolean value that tells you if an element is a directory. Here is how you can use it to only display the files in the current folder:

Command Window

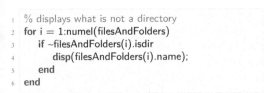

Command Window

```
1  % displays what is not a directory
2  for i = 1:numel(filesAndFolders)
3      if ~filesAndFolders(i).isdir
4          disp(filesAndFolders(i).name);
5      end
6  end
```

```
script1.m
script2.m
textFile1.txt
textFile2.txt
```

2 Generate Files

2.1 Write a Simple File

Here are a few instances of contexts in which a file would be created.

- Automatically define variables in an .m file.

- Automatically generate pieces of code.

- Write .txt documents that contain specific information about a Simulink model (e.g., number of blocks with non-compliant configuration relative to your set of Simulink coding rules)

- Write .txt documents that record information about actions performed by other .m scripts.

Here is the standard way to use the **fopen** function to write to a file:

Content of textFileName.txt

```
1  % 'a' is for appending data to the end of the file
2  % 't' is for opening the file in text mode
3  fid = fopen('textFileName.txt', 'at');
4
5  fprintf(fid, '%s\n', 'Text to write in the text file');
6
7  fclose(fid);
```

```
textFileName.txt  ×  +
1  Text to write in the text file
2  |
```

fileMan/standardTextWriting.m

In this example we used a text file; however, it would have worked just as well with any other extension.

3 Read Files

3.1 Import a Text File into MATLAB Using fgetl

I have written a tutorial on using the **fgetl** function to import a text file, but the truth is, you don't need to read it. The following summary will give you all the tools you need:

1. Read a text file line by line using:

```
while ~feof(fid) % while there is still text to read
        textLineEntry = fgetl(fid) % read a line and go to the next
end
```

2. Store every line of the text file into a variable using a cell array:

```
textLineEntryCellArray = [];
fid = fopen('fileToRead.txt');
while ~feof(fid)
        textLineEntry = fgetl(fid);
        entireTextCellArray = [entireTextCellArray {textLineEntry}];
end
fclose(fid)
```

3. Replace a word in a line using the MATLAB command **strrep**:

```
textLineEntryUpdated = strrep(textLineEntry, oldText, newText);
```

4. Read a line word by word using **strsplit**:

```
words = strsplit(textLineEntry, ' ');
```

5. Cut a line in half using the **strtok** MATLAB command:

```
[token, remain] = strtok(textLineEntry, delimiter);
```

6. Query for the presence of a string value in a line using the **strfind** MATLAB command:

```
keywordPresent = ~isempty(strfind(textLineEntry, keyword));
```

If you do want the full tutorial, you can find it here:

```
https://realtechnologytools.com/read-text-file
```

3.2 Find a Parameter in a .m File

Sometimes you will have to open a file, read it, and replace some text in it. You may have use for this function in order to modify .m files. For example, if you want to switch between Simulink model variants defined in an .m file, or if you want to update the definition of a parameter because it's managed from an outside database, this would be a good way to do that.

We'll use the **fopen** function twice: first to scan a file and then to write another file that is identical to the first file except for the text you want to replace. Once this is done, all you have to do is delete the original file and give the new file the same name as the original file:

```
 1  function replaceInFile(file, oldText, newText)
 2
 3  [fileName, fileExtension] = strtok(file, '.');
 4  scriptFileNew = [fileName '_new' fileExtension];
 5
 6  if exist(scriptFileNew) == 2
 7      delete(scriptFileNew);
 8  end
 9
10  fin = fopen([fileName fileExtension]);
11  fout = fopen(scriptFileNew, 'w');
12
13  previousTxtNotFound = true;
14  while ~feof(fin)
15      textLineEntry = fgetl(fin);
16      if ~isempty(strfind(textLineEntry, oldText))
17          textLineEntry = strrep(textLineEntry, oldText, newText);
18          previousTxtNotFound = false;
19      end
20      fprintf(fout, '%s\n', textLineEntry);
21  end
22
23  fclose(fin);
24  fclose(fout);
25
26  assert(previousTxtNotFound, ['Error occured, ' oldText ' not found in ' fileName ' file.']);
27
28  end
```

fileMan/replaceInFile.m

This function will return an error message if the text to be replaced doesn't appear in the file.

Let's try this function using the file *textFileName.txt*.

```
textFileName_new.txt  ×  +
1  Text replaced in the text file
2
```

```
1  fileName = 'textFileName.txt';
2  oldText = 'to write';
3  newText = 'replaced';
4  replaceInFile(fileName, oldText, newText);
```

fileMan/replaceInFileTestEnvironment.m

There are 2 new MATLAB commands used in *replaceInFile.m*:

- **exist.** It is useful when we want to know if a file or a folder already exists in the current folder. Here are the 2 main ways to use that command, you compare the output to:

7 if it's a folder

```
if exist('folderName')==7
    ...
end
```

2 if it's a file

```
if exist('fileName.ext')==2
    ...
end
```

- **assert.** This command is used as a safety net, it generates an error when something goes wrong. For example, you will always know that the *replaceInFile* function has found the text, otherwise you'd have an error. Therefore, if the output is not what you expected, you know that it's not because the file doesn't contain the text you want to replace. Here's how it works:

No Error Detected

```
>> assert(true, 'Error!');
>>
```

Error Detected

```
>> assert(false, 'Error!');
Error!
```

4   Generate LaTeX Files from MATLAB

4.1   Why Latex?

One reason to use Latex as your preferred tool for automation of document creation is that it's one of the best tools (if not *the* best) for creating documents properly. In this day and age, there's no excuse for writing poorly formatted documents. Latex is also plain text (meaning the formatting is indicated with commands that are entered by typing keyboard characters, as opposed to being embedded in the document as it is in Microsoft Word, for example), which makes it the perfect candidate for automatically generated high-quality documentation.

Most documents are not supposed to be written manually, because most of the information being documented usually already exists in another format and redundancy of information is prohibited when you want consistency, efficiency, and reliability.

If you don't know anything about Latex and you want to know the basics in 5 minutes so that you can create your own Latex template to use for documenting, go to

```
https://realtechnologytools.com/latex-template
```

4.2 Generate a Latex File

In this section, I'll assume that you are already familiar with Latex, to some extent at least, or that you have read the article about the basics of Latex. The following script generates a basic Latex file with the main components for composing a document (a title, sections, subsections, subsubsections, a table of contents, and lists of bullet points):

```
1   % choose the Latex file name
2   filename = 'basicLatexFileGenerated.tex';
3   delete(filename);
4   fid = fopen(filename, 'at');
5
6   fprintf(fid, '%s', ['\documentclass[10pt]{article}' char(10)]);
7   % choose a font for your document
8   fprintf(fid, '%s', ['\usepackage{mathpazo}' char(10) char(10)]);
9   % I will explain the packages below in the next section
10  fprintf(fid, '%s', ['% below, the minimum packages needed to generate the table' char
        (10)]);
11  fprintf(fid, '%s', ['\usepackage{xcolor, colortbl}' char(10)]);
12  fprintf(fid, '%s', ['\usepackage{hyphenat}' char(10)]);
13  fprintf(fid, '%s', ['\usepackage{longtable}' char(10) char(10)]);
14  % write the title of your document
15  fprintf(fid, '%s', ['\title{Generated Latex File}' char(10)]);
16  % remove the date from the title generated with the command \maketitle
17  fprintf(fid, '%s', ['\date{}' char(10)]);
18
19  % begining of your document
20  fprintf(fid, '%s', ['\begin{document}' char(10) char(10)]);
21  % write the title and the table of contents
22  fprintf(fid, '%s', ['\maketitle' char(10)]);
23  fprintf(fid, '%s', ['\tableofcontents' char(10) char(10)]);
24  % write the content of your document
25  fprintf(fid, '%s', ['\section{First section of the document}' char(10)]);
26  fprintf(fid, '%s', ['\subsection{First subsection of the document}' char(10)]);
27  fprintf(fid, '%s', ['\subsubsection{First subsubsection of the document}' char(10)]);
28  fprintf(fid, '%s', ['Here is a list of bullet points generated from MATLAB:' char(10)]);
29  fprintf(fid, '%s', ['\begin{itemize}' char(10)]);
30  fprintf(fid, '%s', ['\item First bullet point' char(10)]);
31  fprintf(fid, '%s', ['\item Second bullet point' char(10)]);
32  fprintf(fid, '%s', ['\end{itemize}' char(10) char(10)]);
33
34  fprintf(fid, '%s', ['\end{document}' char(10)]);
35
36  fclose(fid);
```

fileMan/generateBasicLatexFile.m

From that script, MATLAB generates the Latex file *basicLatexFileGenerated.tex*:

```
 1 \documentclass[10pt]{article}
 2 \usepackage{mathpazo}
 3
 4 % below, the minimum packages needed to generate the table
 5 \usepackage{xcolor, colortbl}
 6 \usepackage{hyphenat}
 7 \usepackage{longtable}
 8
 9 \title{Generated Latex File}
10 \date{}
11 \begin{document}
12
13 \maketitle
14 \tableofcontents
15
16 \section{First section of the document}
17 \subsection{First subsection of the document}
18 \subsubsection{First subsubsection of the document}
19 Here is a list of bullet points generated from MATLAB:
20 \begin{itemize}
21 \item First bullet point
22 \item Second bullet point
23 \end{itemize}
24
25 \end{document}
```

fileMan/basicLatexFileGenerated.tex

There are three packages that are not needed for this basic Latex file generated but that will be needed in the next section, where we'll see how to generate a table:

- \usepackage{xcolor, colortbl}: needed to have color in tables

- \usepackage{longtable}: needed to have a table extends over two or more pages

- \usepackage{hyphenat}: prevents the content of the cells from exceeding the table width

After compiling the basic file twice (so that the table of contents can be generated), the following pdf file will be generated:

Generated Latex File

Contents

1 First section of the document

1.1 First subsection of the document

1.1.1 First subsubsection of the document

Here is a list of bullet points generated from MATLAB:

- First bullet point
- Second bullet point

4.3 Generate a Table

Quite frankly, implementing the **tableTex** function wasn't the most intuitive task in the world. Thus I won't go into much detail as to how it was implemented. Besides, the value of the material presented here lies in the function as a tool, not in the reasoning that went into its implementation.

```
 1  function tableTex(fid, table, header, colorHeader, forcedSize, fontSize)
 2
 3  assert(size(table, 2)==numel(header), ...
 4      'The header of the table is not the same size as the table.');
 5  assert(size(table, 2)==numel(forcedSize), ...
 6      'The forced size is not the same size as the table.');
 7
 8  column = [];
 9  for i = 1:numel(forcedSize)
10      column = [column 'p{' num2str(forcedSize(i)) '\textwidth}|'];
11  end
12  red = num2str(colorHeader(1));
13  green = num2str(colorHeader(2));
14  blue = num2str(colorHeader(3));
15  fprintf(fid, '%s', ['\definecolor{colorTblHeader}{rgb}{' red ',' green ', ' blue '}' char(10)
        ]);
16  fprintf(fid, '%s', ...
17      ['{\' fontSize char(10) '\begin{longtable}{|' column '}' char(10) '\hline' char(10)]);
18  % format the header and write the table
19  formattedHeader = [...
20      {['\multicolumn{1}{|c|}{\cellcolor{colorTblHeader} \textbf{' header{1} '}}']} ...
21      {['\multicolumn{1}{|c|}{\cellcolor{colorTblHeader} \textbf{' header{2} '}}']}];
22  completeTable = [formattedHeader; table];
23  writeArray(fid, completeTable);
24
25  fprintf(fid, '%s', ['\end{longtable}' char(10) '}' char(10)]);
26
27  end
28
29  function writeArray(fid, array)
30
31  for i = 1:size(array, 1)
32      fprintf(fid, '%s', ['    ' array{i, 1}]);
33      for j = 2:size(array, 2)
34          fprintf(fid, '%s', [' & ' array{i, j}]);
35      end
36      fprintf(fid, '%s', ['\\ \hline' char(10)]);
37  end
38
39  end
```

fileMan/tableTex.m

As I said, the goal is to understand how to use this function. This function has 6 arguments:

- **fid**: output of the **fopen** MATLAB function. This means that you have to "open" a file prior to using this function.

- **table**: matrix of strings or characters that you want to create.

- **header**: vector containing the first entry in each column of the table (usually representing the column title)

- **colorHeader**: color of the first line of the table

- **forcedSize**: size of each column relative to full width of the page

- **fontSize**: font size to be used for the content of the table using Latex terminology (i.e., **tiny, scriptsize, footnotesize, small, normalsize, large, Large, LARGE, huge** or **Huge**).

The following script is an example of generation of a two-column Latex table:

```
1  variable1 = 'firstWordInList';
2  variable2 = 'secondWordInList';
3  variable3 = 'thirdWordInList';
4  variable4 = 'fourthWordInList';
5  matrix = [{variable1} {variable2}; {variable3} {variable4}];
6
7  % choose the Latex file name
8  filename = 'latexTable.tex';
9  delete(filename);
10 fid = fopen(filename, 'at');
11
12 header = [{'Name'} {'Description'}];
13 fontSize = 'scriptsize';
14 colorHeader = [0.8 0.8 0.8];      % gray color
15 Column1Width = 0.4;               % width of the first column (1 is full length)
16 totalTableWidth = 0.87;          % width of the full table
17 % convert the size of the columns to make it a percentage of totalTableWidth
18 sizeColumn1 = Column1Width*totalTableWidth;
19 sizeColumn2 = totalTableWidth−sizeColumn1;
20 forcedSize = [sizeColumn1 sizeColumn2];
21
22 tableTex(fid, matrix, header, colorHeader, forcedSize, fontSize);
23
24 fclose(fid);
```

fileMan/latexTableGeneration.m

That script generates the Latex file *latexTable.tex*:

```
1  \definecolor{colorTblHeader}{rgb}{0.8,0.8, 0.8}
2  {\scriptsize
3  \begin{longtable}{|p{0.348\textwidth}|p{0.522\textwidth}|}
4  \hline
5     \multicolumn{1}{|c|}{\cellcolor{colorTblHeader} \textbf{Name}} & \multicolumn
         {1}{|c|}{\cellcolor{colorTblHeader} \textbf{Description}}\\ \hline
6     firstWordInList & secondWordInList\\ \hline
7     thirdWordInList & fourthWordInList\\ \hline
8  \end{longtable}
9  }
```

fileMan/latexTable.tex

You can then re-use the previous script to include the table in a document using the Latex command \input{latexTable.tex}. For the sake of this example, I kept only the title and the first section:

```
1   % choose the Latex file name
2   filename = 'basicLatexTableFile.tex';
3   delete(filename);
4   fid = fopen(filename, 'at');
5
6   fprintf(fid, '%s', ['\documentclass[10pt]{article}' char(10)]);
7   fprintf(fid, '%s', ['\usepackage{mathpazo}' char(10) char(10)]);
8   fprintf(fid, '%s', ['% below, the minimum packages needed to generate the table' char
         (10)]);
9   fprintf(fid, '%s', ['\usepackage{xcolor, colortbl}' char(10)]);
10  fprintf(fid, '%s', ['\usepackage{hyphenat}' char(10)]);
11  fprintf(fid, '%s', ['\usepackage{longtable}' char(10) char(10)]);
12  fprintf(fid, '%s', ['\title{Generated Latex File}' char(10)]);
13  fprintf(fid, '%s', ['\date{}' char(10)]);
14
15  fprintf(fid, '%s', ['\begin{document}' char(10) char(10)]);
16  fprintf(fid, '%s', ['\maketitle' char(10)]);
17  fprintf(fid, '%s', ['\section{First section of the document}' char(10)]);
18  fprintf(fid, '%s', ['This is the table that has been written from MATLAB:' char(10)]);
19
20  % add your table to the file
21  fprintf(fid, '%s', ['\input{latexTable.tex}' char(10) char(10)]);
22  fprintf(fid, '%s', ['\end{document}' char(10)]);
23
24  fclose(fid);
```

fileMan/generateBasicLatexTableFile.m

This generates the Latex file *basicLatexTableFile.tex*:

```
1  \documentclass[10pt]{article}
2  \usepackage{mathpazo}
3
4  % below, the minimum packages needed to include the table generated
5  \usepackage{xcolor, colortbl}
6  \usepackage{hyphenat}
7  \usepackage{longtable}
8
9  \title{Generated Latex File}
10 \date{}
11 \begin{document}
12
13 \maketitle
14
15 \section{First section of the document}
16 This is the table that has been written from MATLAB:
17 \input{latexTable.tex}
18
19 \end{document}
```

fileMan/basicLatexTableFile.tex

Finally, we get

Generated Latex File

1   First section of the document

This is the table that has been written from MATLAB:

Name	Description
firstWordInList	secondWordInList
thirdWordInList	fourthWordInList

Note that the generation of the table and the generation of the document are independent. Why? Because you won't update them at the same frequency. Once you have generated the document, you only need to update the table (*latexTable.tex*) unless the text presenting the table depends on its content.

4.4 Format Your Text for Latex

Obviously, if you generate a table based on information extracted from a database, you will have to format the information so that the generated Latex file does not generate error messages.

If a word contains underscores ("_") or backslashes ("\"), as in the word "firstWord-InList_TO_BE_DEFINED" for example, then you'll have to modify that word before writing it to your Latex file as "firstWordInList_TO_BE_DEFINED" (otherwise, the underscores will be interpreted by Latex as commands). Also, the command for using a backslash in Latex is \textbackslash.

The following function does this for you:

```
1  function strFormatted = formatStrTex(str)
2
3  % get rid of '\', replace them with '\textbackslash'
4  oldText = '\';
5  newText = '\textbackslash ';
6  strFormatted = strrep(str, oldText, newText);
7
8  % use the new text to apply the next replacement
9  str = strFormatted;
10
11 % get rid of '_', replace them with '\_'
12 oldText = '_';
13 newText = '\_';
14 strFormatted = strrep(str, oldText, newText);
15
16 end
```

fileMan/formatStrTex.m

You can apply this function to every cell of a matrix table to make sure the table is well formatted:

```
1  function formattedMatrix = formatMatrixTex(matrix)
2
3  formattedMatrix = [];
4  for i = 1:size(matrix, 1)
5      currentRow = [];
6      for j = 1:size(matrix, 2)
7          currentCell = formatStrTex(matrix{i,j});
8          currentRow = [currentRow {currentCell}];
9      end
10     formattedMatrix = [formattedMatrix; currentRow];
11 end
12
13 end
```

fileMan/formatMatrixTex.m

Again, the value of the material presented here lies in illustrating how to use the function *formatStrTex.m*, so here is the previous example with data requiring the use of *formatStrTex.m*:

```
 1  variable1 = 'firstWordInList_TO_BE_DEFINED';
 2  variable2 = 'secondWordInList_TO_BE_DEFINED';
 3  variable3 = 'thirdWordInList_TO_BE_DEFINED';
 4  variable4 = 'fourthWordInList_TO_BE_DEFINED';
 5  matrix = [{variable1} {variable2}; {variable3} {variable4}];
 6
 7  % format the content of the matrix
 8  formattedMatrix = formatMatrixTex(matrix);
 9
10  filename = 'latexFormattedTable.tex';
11  delete(filename);
12
13  fid = fopen(filename, 'at');
14
15  header = [{'Name'} {'Description'}];
16  fontSize = 'scriptsize';
17  colorHeader = [0.8 0.8 0.8];
18  Column1Width = 0.4;
19  totalTableWidth = 0.87;
20  sizeColumn1 = Column1Width*totalTableWidth;
21  sizeColumn2 = totalTableWidth−sizeColumn1;
22  forcedSize = [sizeColumn1, sizeColumn2];
23
24  tableTex(fid, formattedMatrix, header, colorHeader, forcedSize, fontSize);
25
26  fclose(fid);
```

fileMan/latexFormattedTableGeneration.m

This will generate the file *latexFormattedTable.tex*:

```
1  \definecolor{colorTblHeader}{rgb}{0.8,0.8, 0.8}
2  {\scriptsize
3  \begin{longtable}{|p{0.348\textwidth}|p{0.522\textwidth}|}
4  \hline
5  \multicolumn{1}{|c|}{\cellcolor{colorTblHeader} \textbf{Name}} & \multicolumn
     {1}{|c|}{\cellcolor{colorTblHeader} \textbf{Description}}\\ \hline
6  firstWordInList\_TO\_BE\_DEFINED & secondWordInList\_TO\_BE\_DEFINED
     \\ \hline
7  thirdWordInList\_TO\_BE\_DEFINED & fourthWordInList\_TO\_BE\_DEFINED
     \\ \hline
8  \end{longtable}
9  }
```

fileMan/latexFormattedTable.tex

As you can see, the function seems to have worked well, since every underscore is preceded by a backslash.

Now you can generate a Latex file that inputs *latexFormattedTable.tex*:

```
1  % write down the latex file
2  filename = 'latexFileGeneratedFormattedTable.tex';
3  delete(filename);
4
5  fid = fopen(filename, 'at');
6
7  fprintf(fid, '%s', ['\documentclass[10pt]{article}' char(10)]);
8  fprintf(fid, '%s', ['\usepackage{mathpazo}' char(10) char(10)]);
9
10 fprintf(fid, '%s', ['% below, the minimum packages needed to generate the table' char
      (10)]);
11 fprintf(fid, '%s', ['\usepackage{xcolor, colortbl}' char(10)]);
12 fprintf(fid, '%s', ['\usepackage{hyphenat}' char(10)]);
13 fprintf(fid, '%s', ['\usepackage{longtable}' char(10) char(10)]);
14 fprintf(fid, '%s', ['\title{Generated Latex File}' char(10)]);
15 fprintf(fid, '%s', ['\date{}' char(10)]);
16
17 fprintf(fid, '%s', ['\begin{document}' char(10) char(10)]);
18 fprintf(fid, '%s', ['\maketitle' char(10) char(10)]);
19 fprintf(fid, '%s', ['\section{First section of the document}' char(10)]);
20 fprintf(fid, '%s', ['This is the table that has been written from MATLAB:' char(10)]);
21 fprintf(fid, '%s', ['\input{latexFormattedTable.tex}' char(10) char(10)]);
22 fprintf(fid, '%s', ['\end{document}' char(10)]);
23
24 fclose(fid);
```

fileMan/generateLatexFileFormattedTable.m

That generates the Latex file *latexFileGeneratedFormattedTable.tex*:

```
1  \documentclass[10pt]{article}
2  \usepackage{mathpazo}
3
4  % below, the minimum packages needed to include the table generated
5  \usepackage{xcolor, colortbl}
6  \usepackage{hyphenat}
7  \usepackage{longtable}
8
9  \title{Generated Latex File}
10 \date{}
11 \begin{document}
12
13 \maketitle
14
15 \section{First section of the document}
16 This is the table that has been written from MATLAB:
17 \input{latexFormattedTable.tex}
18
19 \end{document}
```

fileMan/latexFileGeneratedFormattedTable.tex

Generated Latex File

1 First section of the document

This is the table that has been written from MATLAB:

Name	Description
firstWordInList.TO_BE_DEFINED	secondWordInList.TO_BE_DEFINED
thirdWordInList.TO_BE_DEFINED	fourthWordInList.TO_BE_DEFINED

5 Generate Word Documents

5.1 Open a Word Document

In MATLAB , the easiest way to open a Word document is to use the **actxserver** function to create a COM Automation server. Here's how to do it:

```matlab
1  function file = openWord(fullPath, fileName)
2
3  wordPath = fullfile(fullPath, fileName);
4  word = actxserver('Word.Application');
5  document = word.Documents.Open(wordPath);
6
7  file.application = word;
8  file.document = document;
9
10 end
```

fileMan/word/openWord.m

You need 2 input arguments to use this function:

- `fullPath`: the absolute path that leads to where your file is.

- `fileName`: the name (with the extension) of the Word document to open.

The output argument of this function is the structure `file` which consists of the Word application as well as the Word document. If you don't see how they differ, open the Word application and you will see that you can open and close documents without closing the application, that's why we have 2 distinct fields.

5.2 Save and Close a Word Document

We also need to save and close the Word document when we are done with it:

```matlab
1  function closeWord(file, save)
2
3  word = file.application;
4  document = file.document;
5
6  document.Close(save); % close the document
7  word.Quit; % close word
8  delete(word); % delete server object
9
10 end
```

fileMan/word/closeWord.m

You can use the **closeWord** function as the following:

- `closeWord(file, true)`: saves the document before closing it.

- `closeWord(file, false)`: closes the document without saving.

5.3 Write Text in a Word Document

5.3.1 Standard Example

```
1   % 1. open Activex server
2   fullPath = pwd;
3   fileName = 'wordTestFile.docx';
4   file = openWord(fullPath, fileName);
5
6   % 2. process the file
7   document = file.document;
8   document.Content.Text = 'Test.';
9
10  % 3. close word
11  closeWord(file, true);
```

Content of wordTestFile.docx

Test.

fileMan/word/standardWordWriting.m

5.3.2 Generate a Basic Word Document

Here is a template that you can use to generate your own documents. The main elements you will need in a document are: text, titles, headings, tables, and different formatting styles (font, size, colors, ...). You can find all of them in the following template:

```
1   % 1. open Activex server
2   fullPath = pwd;
3   fileName = 'basicWordDocument.docx';
4   file = openWord(fullPath, fileName);
5
6   % 2. process the file
7   word = file.application;
8   word.Visible = true; % make it visibile on the screen
9
10  word.Selection.Style = 'Heading 1'; % enter the style (section, subsection, ...)
11  word.Selection.ParagraphFormat.Alignment = 1;  % center-align the title
12  word.Selection.Font.Size = 35; % change the font size
13  word.Selection.TypeText('Generated Word Document'); % enter the title here
14  word.Selection.TypeParagraph; % press the enter key
15  word.Selection.TypeParagraph;
16  word.Selection.Style = 'Heading 2';
17  word.Selection.Font.Size = 20;
18  word.Selection.TypeText('This Is the First Heading');
19  word.Selection.TypeParagraph;
20  word.Selection.Style = 'Normal';
21  word.Selection.TypeText('Here is some text.');
22  word.Selection.TypeParagraph;
23  word.Selection.Style = 'Heading 2';
24  word.Selection.Font.Size = 20;
25  word.Selection.TypeText('This Is the Second Heading');
26  word.Selection.TypeParagraph;
27  word.Selection.Style = 'Heading 3';
28  word.Selection.Font.Size = 15;
29  word.Selection.TypeText('Here Is a Table');
30  word.Selection.TypeParagraph;
31
32  % create a table
33  word.Selection.Style = 'Normal';
34  table = word.Selection.Tables.Add(word.Selection.Range, 3, 2, 1, 1); % insert a table
35  table.Rows.Alignment = 'wdAlignRowCenter'; % center the table
36
37  % define a color for the table header
38  R = 204;
39  G = 204;
40  B = 204;
41  digit = 2; % number of digits in the hexadecimal number
42  BGRHex = [dec2hex(B, digit) dec2hex(G, digit) dec2hex(R, digit)]; % BGR in
        hexadecimal
```

```
43  BGRDec = hex2dec(BGRHex); % BGR in decimal format
44
45  % write the table
46  word.Selection.Shading.BackgroundPatternColor = BGRDec;
47  word.Selection.Font.Bold = true;
48  word.Selection.TypeText('My');
49  word.Selection.MoveRight;
50  word.Selection.Shading.BackgroundPatternColor = BGRDec;
51  word.Selection.Font.Bold = true;
52  word.Selection.TypeText('Table');
53  word.Selection.MoveRight;
54  word.Selection.TypeText('A');
55  word.Selection.MoveRight;
56  word.Selection.TypeText('B');
57  word.Selection.MoveRight;
58  word.Selection.TypeText('C');
59  word.Selection.MoveRight;
60  word.Selection.TypeText('D');
61
62  % 3. close word
63  closeWord(file, true);
```

fileMan/word/generateBasicWordDocument.m

In this example, we define the word variable as the application field of the file structure. We then use the Selection object word.Selection which represents the insertion point in the document.

It's worth mentioning here that the definition of colors in MATLAB is a bit tricky, we need to convert the usual RGB to BRG using the hexadecimal format. We get:

Generated Word Document

This Is the First Heading
Here is some text.|

This Is the Second Heading
Here Is a Table

My	Table
A	B
C	D

6 Read Word Documents

6.1 Read Text From a Word Document

Now that we know how to generate a basic Word document, let's see how to read this same document paragraph by paragraph.

```matlab
% 1. open Activex server
fullPath = pwd;
fileName = 'basicWordDocument.docx';
file = openWord(fullPath, fileName);

% 2. read data from the Word document
document = file.document;
word = file.application;

for i = 1:document.Range.Paragraphs.Count

    % in matlab  we use collectionName.Item(index) instead of collectionName(index)
    paragraph = word.ActiveDocument.Paragraphs.Item(i);
    textFormatted = paragraph.Range.Text;

    % get the text in the paragraph
    if strcmp(paragraph.Style.NameLocal, 'Heading 1')
        tag = 'HEADING 1';
    elseif strcmp(paragraph.Style.NameLocal, 'Heading 2')
        tag = 'HEADING 2';
    elseif strcmp(paragraph.Style.NameLocal, 'Heading 3')
        tag = 'HEADING 3';
    else
        tag = 'NO TAG';
    end
    disp([tag ': ' textFormatted]);
end

% 3. close word
closeWord(file, true);
```

fileMan/word/readTextFromWordDocument.m

We get:

```
HEADING 1: Generated Word Document

NO TAG:

HEADING 2: This Is the First Heading

NO TAG: Here is some text.

HEADING 2: This Is the Second Heading

HEADING 3: Here Is a Table

NO TAG: My
□
NO TAG: Table
□
NO TAG:
□
NO TAG: A
□
NO TAG: B
□
NO TAG:
□
NO TAG: C
□
NO TAG: D
□
NO TAG: |
□
NO TAG:
```

Here are the important elements of this script:

- `document.Range.Paragraphs.Count`: number of paragraphs in the document.

- `word.ActiveDocument.Paragraphs.Item(i)`: the ith paragraph in the document (you need to refer to the index of an object using the `Item` method) .

- `paragraph.Style.NameLocal`: used to identify the type of headings we are using.

Note that every cell of the table is a paragraph and is thus read using this method. Also, aside from the square symbols (used as a delimiter for the cells), there's no tag for the table. We'll see in the next section how to add this tag.

6.2 Read a Table From a Word Document: Range.Text

```
1   % 1. open Activex server
2   fullPath = pwd;
3   fileName = 'basicWordDocument.docx';
4   file = openWord(fullPath, fileName);
5
6   % 2. read data from the Word document
7   document = file.document;
8   word = file.application;
9
10  i = 1;
11  % we use a while loop because we'll jump when displaying the entire table
12  while i <= document.Range.Paragraphs.Count
13      % in matlab  we use collectionName.Item(index) instead of collectionName(index)
14      paragraph = word.ActiveDocument.Paragraphs.Item(i);
15
16      % identify tables
17      paragraphRangeIsInTable = paragraph.Range.Tables.Count > 0;
18      textFormatted = paragraph.Range.Text;
19
20      % get the text in the paragraph
21      if paragraphRangeIsInTable
22          % get the reference to the table
23          table = paragraph.Range.Tables.Item(1);
24          numberOfRows = table.Rows.Count;
25          numberOfColumns = table.Columns.Count;
26          tag = ['[' num2str(numberOfRows) 'x' num2str(numberOfColumns) '] TABLE'];
27
28          % Word uses two characters as a sepearator in a table
29          textFormatted = textFormatted(1:end-2);
30
31      elseif strcmp(paragraph.Style.NameLocal, 'Heading 1')
32          tag = 'HEADING 1';
33      elseif strcmp(paragraph.Style.NameLocal, 'Heading 2')
34          tag = 'HEADING 2';
35      elseif strcmp(paragraph.Style.NameLocal, 'Heading 3')
36          tag = 'HEADING 3';
37      else
38          tag = 'NO TAG';
39      end
40      disp([tag ': ' textFormatted]);
41      i = i + 1;
42  end
43
44  % 3. close word
45  closeWord(file, true);
```

fileMan/word/readTableWithRangeText.m

We get:

```
HEADING 1: Generated Word Document

NO TAG:

HEADING 2: This Is the First Heading

NO TAG: Here is some text.

HEADING 2: This Is the Second Heading

HEADING 3: Here Is a Table

[3x2] TABLE: My
[3x2] TABLE: Table
[3x2] TABLE:
[3x2] TABLE: A
[3x2] TABLE: B
[3x2] TABLE:
[3x2] TABLE: C
[3x2] TABLE: D
[3x2] TABLE:
NO TAG:
```

We used:

- `paragraph.Range.Tables.Count > 0`: to identify when a paragraph was in a table.

- `paragraph.Range.Tables.Item(1)`: to access the table that we were in.

- `table.Rows.Count`: to get the number of rows of a table.

- `table.Columns.Count`: to get the number of columns of a table.

- `textFormatted = textFormatted(1:end-2)`: to get rid of the cell delimiters.

As you can see, an empty paragraph marks the end of a row. Also, using this method, we don't really know when the table starts and ends.

Ideally, we'd like to display the entire table as soon as we see that a paragraph is in a table. We would then be able to process the tables and the "regular" paragraphs separately, we'll see how to do that in the next section.

6.3   Read a Table From a Word Document: Range.Tables

We already know how to identify a table, let's see how to display it:

```
1   % 1. open Activex server
2   fullPath = pwd;
3   fileName = 'basicWordDocument.docx';
4   file = openWord(fullPath, fileName);
5
6   % 2. read data from the Word document
7   document = file.document;
8   word = file.application;
9
10  i = 1;
11  % we use a while loop because we'll jump when displaying the entire table
12  while i <= document.Range.Paragraphs.Count
13
14      % in matlab  we use collectionName.Item(index) instead of collectionName(index)
15      paragraph = word.ActiveDocument.Paragraphs.Item(i);
16
17      % identify tables
18      paragraphRangeIsInTable = paragraph.Range.Tables.Count > 0;
19
20      % get the text in the paragraph
21      if paragraphRangeIsInTable
22          % get the reference to the table
23          table = paragraph.Range.Tables.Item(1);
24          i = displayEntireTable(table, i);
25      elseif strcmp(paragraph.Style.NameLocal, 'Heading 1')
26          textFormatted = paragraph.Range.Text;
27          tag = 'HEADING 1';
28          disp([tag ': ' textFormatted]);
29      elseif strcmp(paragraph.Style.NameLocal, 'Heading 2')
30          textFormatted = paragraph.Range.Text;
31          tag = 'HEADING 2';
32          disp([tag ': ' textFormatted]);
33      elseif strcmp(paragraph.Style.NameLocal, 'Heading 3')
34          textFormatted = paragraph.Range.Text;
35          tag = 'HEADING 3';
36          disp([tag ': ' textFormatted]);
37      else
38          tag = 'NO TAG';
39          disp([tag ': ' textFormatted]);
40      end
41      i = i + 1;
42  end
43
44  % 3. close word
45  closeWord(file, true);
```

fileMan/word/readTableWithRangeTables.m

```
 1  function indexUpdated = displayEntireTable(table, index)
 2
 3  numberOfRows = table.Rows.Count;
 4  numberOfColumns = table.Columns.Count;
 5  for i = 1:numberOfRows
 6    for j = 1:numberOfColumns
 7      textFormatted = table.Cell(i, j).Range.Text;
 8      % Word uses two characters as a separator in a table
 9      textFormatted = textFormatted(1:end-2);
10      disp(['C(' num2str(i) ', ' num2str(j) ') ' textFormatted]);
11    end
12  end
13
14  indexUpdated = index + numberOfRows*numberOfColumns + numberOfRows;
15
16  end
```

fileMan/word/displayEntireTable.m

We get:

```
HEADING 1: Generated Word Document

NO TAG: Generated Word Document

HEADING 2: This Is the First Heading

NO TAG: This Is the First Heading

HEADING 2: This Is the Second Heading

HEADING 3: Here Is a Table

C(1, 1) My
C(1, 2) Table
C(2, 1) A
C(2, 2) B
C(3, 1) C
C(3, 2) D
```

In the **displayEntireTable** function, we use the reference to the table as an input argument to read each cell inside. We also have to update the index i that counts the paragraphs so that the next iteration of the while-loop refers to the paragraph that comes right after the table.

7 Key Takeways

(1) Stay organized with the documents you generate, using the MATLAB commands **movefile, copyfile, mkdir, rmdir,** and **clock.**

(2) Use the **dir** MATLAB command to read all files in a folder.

(3) Automatically generate and modify files, using the MATLAB commands **fopen, fclose, fprintf,** and the function **replaceInFile.**

(4) Use **assert** as a safety net in your code.

(5) Compare the output of the MATLAB command **exist** to 7 to know if a folder exists and to 2 to know if a file exists.

(6) Use the function **strrep** to modify a word in a line.

(7) Automatically generate Latex files based on *generateBasicLatexFile.m.*

(8) Use the function **tableTex** to generate tables for Latex with **formatStrTex** when writing information from an outside source, to make sure the generated Latex file won't contain any errors.

Part IV
User Interface

1   Ask the User from the Workspace

To make your macros more user friendly, you may want to have a user interface (this is especially useful when you want to share macros). To do so, you'll need to display a message on the workspace and wait for the user to input their answer using the MATLAB command **input**:

Command Window

```
1  prompt = 'Input argument: \n';
2  inputArgument = input(prompt)
```

userInt/standardPrompt.m

```
>> standardPrompt
Input argument:
|
```

The variable "inputArgument" is the user's answer to the query displayed by the "prompt" variable.

1. Input the Argument

```
>> standardPrompt
Input argument:
85|
```

2. Press the Enter Key

```
>> standardPrompt
Input argument:
85

inputArgument =

   85
```

2   Find a File

Sometimes, you'll need to have the user find a file that's needed for the macro to work. For example, you might need to have the user find a particular Excel file. To do this, you can use the command **uigetfile**:

```
1  extensions = {'*.xlsx';'*.xls'};
2  dialogBoxTitle = 'Choose an Excel file';
3  defaultFile = 'defaultExcelFileName';
4  [fileName, pathName, ~] = uigetfile(extensions, dialogBoxTitle, defaultFile);
```

userInt/standardUIGetFile.m

Since the first two outputs of this function are the main ones, I won't go into detail about the third one (which I've personally never used):

- **fileName:** name of the file selected by the user.

- **pathName:** path of the file selected by the user.

The three input arguments are:

- **extensions:** specifies the extensions of the files that will be displayed in the dialog box.

- **dalogBoxTitle:** title of the dialog box that will appear.

- **defaultFile:** name of the file that will be displayed by default in the dialog box.

3 Ask the User via a GUI

You can also use a GUI (Graphical User Interface) to input arguments:

```
1  % dialog box text
2  prompt = [{'First Argument'}; {'Second Argument'}];
3  % title of the dialog box
4  dlgTitle = 'Version numbers';
5  list = inputdlg(prompt, dlgTitle)
```

userInt/standardGUI.m

Running this script, we get

1. Input the Arguments

2. Click on OK

```
>> standardGUI

list =

    2x1 cell array

        '456'
        '43'
```

4 Externalize Your User Interface Information

4.1 Store Input Arguments

If you know that the frequency with which you'll use your macro will be much higher than the frequency with which the input arguments will vary, you may want to externalize them and update them only when needed.

This also allows for better consistency of information among the macros using the same input arguments (e.g., location of a file, name of a file that changes every time it's updated, reference ID number relative to a model version). You can do this with a separate macro that creates an Excel file in which the arguments will be stored.

Here is an example of how to query for arguments to be stored in an Excel file in the current location:

```
1  function storeArgumentsInExcelFile(excelFileName)
2  % We are using numbers as input for this function to make it more generic
3
4  prompt = 'What is the first argument to be stored?\n';
5  % char(39) is a single quotation mark, it defines a string data type instead of a number
      in Excel
6  firstInputArgument = [char(39) num2str(input(prompt))];
7
8  prompt = 'What is the second argument to be stored?\n';
9  secondInputArgument = [char(39) num2str(input(prompt))];
10
11 matrix = [...
12    {['Reference Information for Inputs.']}, {['']}...
13    ;{firstInputArgument}, {'First argument stored'}...
14    ;{secondInputArgument}, {'Second argument stored'}...
15    ];
16
17 sheetNumber = 1;
18 rowOffset = 0;
19 columnOffset = 0;
20 excelFilePath = pwd;
21 store_matrix(excelFileName, sheetNumber, matrix, excelFilePath, rowOffset,
      columnOffset);
22 winopen(excelFileName);
23
24 end
```

userInt/storeArgumentsInExcelFile.m

As you can see, this function calls **storeMatrix**, which means that MATLAB has to be able to access the *storeMatrix.m* file. You can use **addpath** to do this:

```
1  excelFileName = 'excelFile.xlsx';
2  % add the path to the store_matrix function
3  addpath('../excel');
4  storeArgumentsInExcelFile(excelFileName);
```

userInt/storeInputArguments.m

In this example, we are running *storeInputArguments.m* to store the arguments 456 and 43 in the Excel file *excelFile.xlsx*:

1. Input the Arguments

```
>> storeInputArguments
What is the first argument te be stored?
456
What is the second argument to be stored?
43
```

2. Content of excelFile.xlsx

	A	B	C	D
1	Reference Information for Inputs.			
2	456	First argument stored		
3	43	Second argument stored		

4.2   Get Input Arguments

In order to access the arguments you stored, you need a second function—one that reads the Excel file and looks at the column which references the content that was created from the query (the second column in this example) to locate the desired arguments.

This allows for modification of the function that stores your input arguments, namely *storeArgumentsInExcelFile.m*, so you can change the location of the arguments by moving rows within the Excel file, or by inserting new rows or deleting existing rows (i.e., by modifying *storeArgumentsInExcelFile.m*) without affecting the function you're using to access them:

```matlab
function [firstArgument, secondArgument] = getInputFromExcelFile(fileName)

sheetNumber = 1;
[~, txt, ~] = xlsread(fileName, sheetNumber);

refInfoColumn = txt(2:end, 1);
descriptionColumn = txt(2:end, 2);

% use the value -1 if an argument is not found
firstArgument = '-1';
secondArgument = '-1';
for i = 1:numel(descriptionColumn)
    if strcmp(descriptionColumn(i), 'First argument stored')
        firstArgument = refInfoColumn{i};
    end
    if strcmp(descriptionColumn(i), 'Second argument stored')
        secondArgument = refInfoColumn{i};
    end
end

% generate an error if an argument has not been found
argumentsFound=~((str2num(firstArgument)==-1)||(str2num(secondArgument)
    ==-1));
assert(argumentsFound, ['Issue in ' fileName ', an argument has not been found.']);

end
```

userInt/getInputFromExcelFile.m

We get

```
>> excelFileName = 'excelFile';
>> [firstArgument, secondArgument] = getInputFromExcelFile(excelFileName)

firstArgument =

456


secondArgument =

43
```

5 Key Takeaways

(1) Make your macro more user friendly by using **input** to ask for arguments from the workspace.

(2) Use **uigetfile** to ask a user to find a file.

(3) Use **inputdlg** to ask for arguments via a GUI.

(4) Externalize your input argument when you frequently use a given macro and the input arguments are almost always the same, or when you need to update input arguments in several functions at once.

Part V

Best Practices in MATLAB: Improve Your Programming Skills

1 Structure Your Projects: Making Things Easy

1.1 Organizing Your Code

1.1.1 Using a Single File

For small projects, the best way I found to organize code in MATLAB is to use most of the functions in a single file, so that the functions contained in this file will be found prior to any functions that aren't in the file. If you have other .m files that contain functions with the same name as the functions in your main file, MATLAB won't take those files into account. Accordingly, you'll be able to modify any function outside of your main one freely with no risk of affecting it.

The only functions that you don't have to group together with your main ones are the functions that have very specific and well-defined roles that you know will not change or require additional input or output (e.g., **storeMatrix**). The reason for this is that if you use a function in different files, maintaining it will be difficult, considering that every improvement or modification of that function will engender the risk of damaging all the other files in which it's involved, since you won't know the impact of the modifications you've made. That's why I usually place my frequently used functions in a particular folder, and then copy and paste them into the file I'm working on when needed.

Now if you want to use a more recent version of your function in your main file you can always do that by updating the corresponding piece of code (by copying and pasting it from your more recent version of it). However, keep in mind that if you do this, you'll have to test it afterwards; otherwise, you'll have no way of making sure that the modifications you've made will have the effect you wanted (and without introducing bugs into your code).

1.1.2 Using Multiple Files

For large projects, placing all of your functions in a single file may not be a good idea. Certainly, if you put too many functions together, the readability and maintainability of your code will be greatly hindered. Instead, you can create separate files and folders to organize your functions by theme. Besides, you can't test your functions independently when they are all in a single file (you can test only the main function in the file, i.e., the function that has the same name as the file). Therefore, you may want to use folders to create some kind of structure for your project. However, if you do this, be careful not to take the functions that are in a given folder and use them in other projects or other functions that have nothing to do with what you're currently doing. Again, if you want to do this, you should copy and paste the file from that folder into your new project, so that it's "frozen" within the context of your current project. If you want to do this, a MATLAB command that's very useful for this purpose is **addpath**.

Suppose you are in the folder named "matlab" that's provided with this book and contains all the code used in the book:

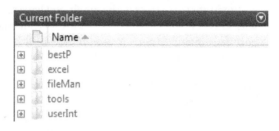

You can use **addpath** to another folder, such as "tools," to add it to the search path (i.e., the paths that MATLAB will look for when you call a function):

```
addpath('tools');
```

bestP/addpathExample.m

Then you will have the following:

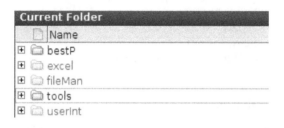

As you can see the "bestP" folder has been added to the search path as well, the reason being that the example code *addpathExample.m* used in this example is located in the "bestP" folder, so I had to add it to the search path to use it.

1.2 Using Shortcuts

Using a button to automate a set of daily tasks that you'll inevitably have to perform is essentially what shortcuts are for in MATLAB. Let's take the trivial example of opening an Excel file.

Let's say the desired Excel file is *excelTestFile.xlsx* located in the "matlab/excel" folder provided with this book. In the absence of a shortcut, you would have to first open your Windows Explorer, then find the Excel file, and finally double-click on the file. Alternatively, you can define the following shortcut:

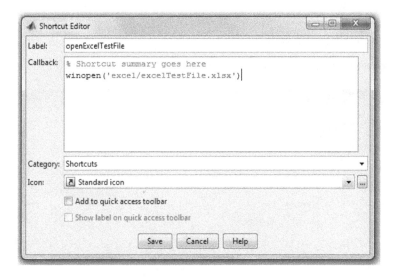

Then you need only to click on the "openExcelFile" shortcut[1] every time you want to open this file:

---

[1]Notice that for this shortcut to work, you have to be in the "matlab" folder provided with this book.

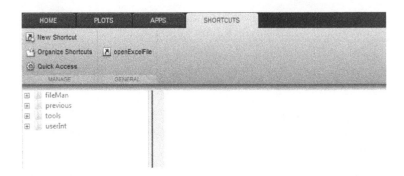

The minor, routine tasks you need to perform are particularly well-suited for short-cuts because of the unnecessary sequences of actions you need to take to perform them as you work.

1.2.1 Creating a Shortcut

To create a shortcut, click on "New Shortcut" in the "SHORTCUTS" tab:

If you don't have the "SHORTCUTS" tab, click on the shortcut icon which is located on the quick access toolbar (in the upper-right corner of your screen). That will enable you to create a new shortcut:

Then, give your new shortcut a name using the "Label" description field. (I usually use the name of the main function called, but you can give it any name you want.)

On the first line of your shortcut definition, I recommend using the **addpath** MATLAB command, which will **add a path to the place where your function is located.** This way you can be sure that your function can be used properly.

On the second line of your shortcut, you may want to **move to the appropriate location** using the **cd** MATLAB command.[2] Admittedly, this line is not mandatory, and you may think "well, I'll just go to this location manually every time I want to use this shortcut," but I recommend including this line whenever there is no downside associated with doing so.

The third line would be **the definition of the arguments of your function.** Defining variables with meaningful names here will also serve as a reminder of how your function is to be used. At the time at which you code the function, it may be difficult to imagine that you'll forget what the arguments are for. Sometime down the line, however (a month from now, two months from now, or a year from now), I can guarantee you that you won't remember the purpose of all of the arguments of all the functions defined.

Finally, the fourth line consists of **calling your main function.**

Here is an example of a shortcut definition that follows the recommendations given above:

---

[2]Notice that in the example, I used relative path for **addpath** and for **cd**, because your absolute path wouldn't be the same as mine, but under normal circumstances I would actually use absolute path in most cases.

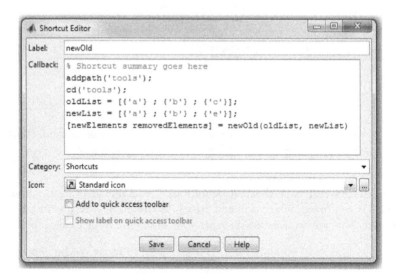

If you define this shortcut and use it in the "matlab" folder that contains all the scripts and functions discussed in this book, you will get

To sum up, here is the procedure to follow:

(Step 1) Make sure you are in the right location using cd(path).

(Step 2) Add your path to the search path using addpath(path).

(Step 3) Define your arguments.

(Step 4) Call your function.

1.2.2   Organizing Your Shortcuts

If you create a shortcut for every function you write, you could easily end up accumulating a large number of shortcuts. You can organize your shortcuts into separate categories as follows:

1. Click on "Organize Shortcuts":

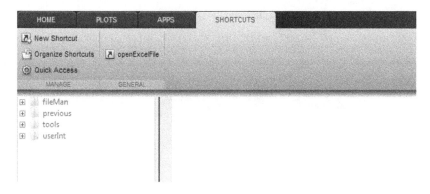

2. Click on "New Category..." to give a name to the category, such as "Excel":

3. Use the drop-down menu to choose the category for your shortcut:

Alternatively, you can use the "Shortcut Organizer" to drag and drop the shortcuts that you've already defined.

1.2.3 Backup, Import, or Export Your Shortcuts

Obviously, backing up your shortcuts and importing/exporting them from one computer to another is paramount if you want your environment to be reliable and movable. Here is the procedure to follow:

(**Step 1**) Use **winopen(prefdir)**, which will open the folder that contains your shortcuts.

(**Step 2**) Backup, import, or export the file **shortcuts_2.xml**, which contains your shortcuts.

(**Step 3**) Backup, import, or export the file **MATLABQuickAccess.xml**, which contains your quick access toolbar shortcuts.

1.3 Using pcode

A .p file is a file which contains code that cannot be read or modified by anyone.

One advantage of using a .p file is that if you have several functions with the same name, MATLAB will find and execute the pcode first. Another advantage is that it will ensure that you are the one who is managing the evolution of your code if you have shared it. Obviously, it can also be used to prevent anyone from seeing how you coded your function.

You can generate a .p file using the MATLAB command **pcode**:

```
1  % this will create a file called "fileToConvert.p"
2  pcode 'fileToConvert.m'
```

bestP/pcodeCreation.m

2 Best Practices for Better Programming in MAT-LAB

2.1 The Most Frequently Used Keyboard Shortcuts of the MAT-LAB Editor

If you use the MATLAB editor, one of the best ways to dramatically improve your productivity with the least investment of time is to learn the MATLAB keyboard shortcuts. The gain in efficiency you'll realize from internalizing them will both enable you to save time and improve your facility in coding. Here are the most frequently used keyboard shortcuts (in order of frequency of use):

1. **F5:** run an entire script.

2. **CTRL+I:** indent the highlighted code.

3. **CTRL+R:** comment code (to insert a % to the left of the code you've highlighted).

4. **CTRL+T:** uncomment code (to delete a % to the left of the code you've highlighted).

5. **CTRL+D:** open the .m file that corresponds to the highlighted file name (e.g., the name of a function).

6. **F9:** run the highlighted piece of code in a script.

7. **CTRL+C:** stop the execution of a code.

8. **ALT+UP/DOWN:** jump from one instance of a variable to another. This is useful for indicating the context in which a variable is used.

9. **CTRL+N/CTRL+W:** open a new script/close the current script.

10. **CTRL+ENTER:** run a cell delimited by %%.

2.2 Writing Clean Scripts

When you write a script, there are a few things that you have to be careful about. First, you want to make sure that the variables you're working with are always the same (i.e., that they don't depend on what's been done in the workspace). To do this, you would use the MATLAB command **clear all**.

You may also want to close all figures and current models that were opened (either manually or by a previous script), by using the MATLAB commands **close all** and **bdclose all**. The classical example of issues that could arise from not taking this precaution is when you have opened a model that initializes itself by using a callback to an .m file when it opens. If you open this model from a script, the outcome will vary, depending on whether or not it was opened before running the script. For example, if the model was opened before running a script that successively removes all variables in your workspace and opens the model, then the model will not open, the callback will not run, and the model will not be initialized. Be careful, however, because the **bdclose all** command closes all models **unconditionally** (so make sure you save it before running the script).

Likewise, you may want to clean up what's displayed in the workspace, by using the **clc** command; otherwise, you won't know if what is displayed stems from the script you just ran or from the previous run of this script (or even from another script you ran).

Lastly, when your script generates other files, make sure to delete those files at the beginning of the script, by using the MATLAB command **delete**; otherwise, you run the risk of using an existing file instead of generating a new one.

To make things simple, this is what I use to start virtually all my scripts:

```
1  % clear the workspace from a script
2  clear all ; close all ; bdclose all ; clc
3
4  % delete the file(s) generated by the script
5  delete('fileName.txt');
```

bestP/scriptExample.m

If the file exists, it will be deleted. If it doesn't, you'll get the following warning message:

```
Warning: File 'fileName.txt' not found.
> In scriptExample at 5
```

A function in MATLAB has its own worskpace; therefore, clearing the worskpace wouldn't work if you use the commands discussed above. You would need to specify the workspace you want to use. In that context, you would have to use the MATLAB command **evalin** as follows:

```
1  % clear the workspace from a function
2  evalin('base', 'clear all; close all; bdclose all; clc')
```

bestP/evalinExample.m

2.3 Using structures

Structures are a way to organize variables and make your code cleaner. Again, I will only give you the basic knowledge for you to start using them right away. Here, the name of the structure is `structureNm`.

1. To define a structure, using a dot (.) after the name of a variable:

```
structureNm.fieldNm1 = valueOne;
structureNm.fieldNm2 = valueTwo;
```

2. To access an element of a structure:

```
structureNm.fieldNm1 % access valueOne
structureNm.fieldNm2 % access valueTwo
```

3. To define an array of structure:

```
i = 1;
structureNm(i).fieldNm = valueOne; % 1st element of the array
i = i+1;
structureNm(i).fieldNm = valueTwo; % 2nd element of the array
i = i+1;
structureNm(i).fieldNm = valueThree; % 3rd element of the array
```

4. To access an element in a structure array:

```
structureNm(elementIndex).fieldNm % access the value of one element
```

5. Here are some useful functions:

```
isfield(structureNm, fieldNm) % 1 if fieldNm is a field, 0 otherwise
fieldnames(structureNm) % returns the names of the fields
isstruct(structureNm) % 1 if structureNm is a structure, 0 otherwise
```

6. To define a nested function:

```
structureNm.fieldNmLevelOne.fieldNmLevelTwo = valueOne;
```

If you do want the full tutorial, you can find it here:

https://realtechnologytools.com/matlab-struct

2.4 Writing Code That Leverages Your Time

Make your code understandable and easy to adapt to other purposes. You have to become an expert at re-purposing your code. The reason why you may consider spending time to make your code as readable and easy to modify as possible is that in the long run it's faster to do it this way. Let's put it this way: The return on investment of the time you put into the development of a macro could be substantial, but the return on the time it would take for you to understand a function in order to tweak and debug it once it's been coded may be less than desirable. Aside from the debugging part, your code will most likely be (at least partially) re-usable in another context. Every time you set out to modify your code, your initial investment will yield dividends in terms of the amount of time you would need to spend in modifying it if you had not invested in the quality of the code at the outset.

Likewise, the goal of automation is to do things once and not have to do them again. However, if you don't put any thought into the way you code and don't try to make it readable for later purposes, re-coding may seem better than re-using existing code, but you'll end up coding the same lines of code over and over again.

In order to code faster, you may want to look at coding as a structure you're building, every piece of code being a tool for future uses. Obviously, you craft every tool for a specific purpose at a specific time, but that doesn't prevent you from considering the possibility of building another tool in the future by combining the ones you've already made. Ideally, you should never start a new function from scratch. You should use all of the tools that you've built and incorporate them into that new function. Viewing every piece of code not as a destination but as part of a greater purpose is one of the best ways I've discovered for writing code that leverages time.

2.5 Best Practical Approaches to Coding

The following is a list of the best practical approaches that I've learned for coding in MATLAB—things that you may want to keep in mind while coding:

1. **Use shortcuts for actions you do frequently.** Aside from the benefits already described, shortcuts may serve as reminders of the variety of functions available for you to use. Also, use the quick access toolbar for the functions that you use frequently (i.e., several times a day). Keep in mind that sometimes the simplest functions can save you a lot of time (e.g., functions that move your location from one folder to another).

2. **Use scripts for testing and functions for developing.** Using a script when you want to develop and automate a task can be a big mistake, because when you want to re-purpose that script for another project, you'll most likely want to make a function out of this script. Bear in mind that, in terms of interaction with the workspace, the differences between a function and a script may make this a non-trivial task.

3. **Spend less time debugging by detecting your errors faster.** When writing code, bear in mind that the more reusable your code is, the faster it will become robust and reliable. If your code can be used in a variety of situations, you'll encounter a broader range of errors than if you use it for a single purpose. Besides, if you can use it in more situations, you'll use it more often and increase your chances of detecting errors.

4. **Merge the testing phase with the development phase.** You may want to consider integrating the testing phase into the development phase, by which I mean continuously comparing what you think you have been doing against what you have actually been coding. The earlier you test your code the better, because the longer you wait before testing your function the more difficult it's going to be to correct the mistakes you've made. Knowing where to look will become more difficult as time goes by, because you may not be able to tell which particular subfunction the error comes from.

5. **Do not write the same piece of information twice.** For example, if you have a piece of information written on a Simulink model, it may be better to avoid copying it from your model to an Excel document. Since the time has already been spent on documenting this information, using your time to copy and paste the information from one place to another seems less efficient and more error-prone than automating the process to begin with. Likewise, when pieces of code greatly resemble each other, you may want to spend some time trying to create a subfunction that uses the information which doesn't vary from one piece of code to another.

6. **Write the closing statement right after writing the opening statement.** For example, if you use an opening bracket, writing the closing bracket would be the second step and writing the content within the brackets would be only the third step. You can follow the same logic for while loops, for loops, if statements, switch statements, functions, fopen commands, braces, and parentheses.

7. **Use version numbers when sharing your code.** If you plan on sharing a function, displaying a version number on the screen every time your func-

tion is executed prevents you from spending time to figure out whether or not the user has the latest version of your function when a bug is detected. The bug may be one that you've already fixed in a more recent version. Here is an example of how to do this:

```
1  versionNumber = 'v4.93';
2  display(['Current version: ' versionNumber])
```

```
>> displayVersionNumber
Current version: v4.93
```

bestP/displayVersionNumber.m

Alternatively, you can use comments at the beginning of the code to indicate when the code was last modified and the name of the person that did the last modification.

8. **Copy and paste your variables when you need to use a variable that's already been defined.** Every time you type a variable that's already been defined, you risk adding a typing mistake to your script. This kind of mistake can be avoided simply by copying and pasting the needed variable. When reading through text, the human brain tends to associate what it understands with what is written on the screen and skip the little mistakes. This is why it can be so difficult to find these mistakes.

9. **Do not have self-imposed limitations.** Bear in mind that there is no risk in automating tasks for which you cannot afford to make mistakes **if** you take the proper precautions. In this case, you may consider the following precautions (obviously, some of these precautions may need to be taken only when you first set out to automate a task, that is, until your code is reliable enough to drop them):

   - Track the actions performed by your code in a separate file (Excel, LaTeX, plain text, Microsoft Word) in order to make sure your code didn't do anything crazy.
   - Manually check everything that has been done by your function (for example, if your code modifies a file, carefully check the file after running your code).
   - If possible, do manually what your code has done and compare.
   - Create a separate macro to check the end result (for example, make sure the output has no redundancies if there's a list of strings where there shouldn't be one).

3 Conclusion: Where to Start

The point of this last section is to help you to get started and to know what to focus on going forward, depending on how much you've already automated. You may want to work on just one of the following ideas until you're done with it before going on to the next one, in order to get the full benefit of each one. Here is a list of the best ideas about what to automate:

- **Your favorite locations.** I won't go on and on about this, as I've already touched on it in the earlier sections, but the first tasks you may want to think of when it comes to automation are the different locations to which you move when you use the **cd** MATLAB command. This is easy and fast to automate and will enable you to begin reaping the benefits of automation right away.

- **Files you open every day.** Think about an Excel, LaTeX, Microsoft Word or .text file you open every day. Use the **winopen** MATLAB command, and create a shortcut so that you can easily access it.

- **Your procedures.** Procedures such as:

    1. Rename file A as B
    2. Create folder C
    3. Move file B into folder C
    4. ...

    The point of writing procedures is so that you can do a complicated task faster and without mistakes. This is basically the first step in automation. Writing a procedure is really fast to do and will save you time in and of itself. But once you've made every step of a procedure really clear and easy to follow, automation of the steps of this procedure is the natural next step. If you don't have the time to automate a very long procedure, start by automating a single step and build on it.

- **Your documentation.** Automating the documentation that you provide on a daily, weekly, or monthly basis is obviously one of the major ideas presented in this book. The easiest document to automate using this book would be a comparison document, for example a document that compares the content of two Excel files (using the **getSelectedColumns** function to extract the content and the **newOld** function to compare them) and writes the differences in a LaTeX file (or in a third Excel file, or even in plain text).

- **Your tests.** Assuming that your test is a script, automating it means having the possibility to run your script (which calls the function you want to test) twice in a row without requiring any manual action in between (e.g., going back to your initial location or removing unnecessarily generated files). For example, if every time you run your script you have to restore a previous version of a file (i.e., remove the current file and copy and paste a previous version) because your function modified it, then testing your macros will be too much of a hassle for you to systematically run your tests, which will prevent you from comparing what you think you've been doing against what you've actually been doing.

- **Your checks.** An easy example of a check would be simply to open an Excel file at the end of a function that modified it. This can be done using the **winopen** MATLAB command. An example of a more sophisticated check—one that would be helpful if you're manipulating a list of cells that would ultimately end up in an Excel file—could consist of comparing the initial number of cells to the number of cells in the Excel file. If those two numbers are the same, the check would be easy to code, but if that isn't the case you may want to create a check that uses a different method to calculate the resulting cells. Bear in mind that in this example, the resulting number of cells has to be determined in a manner that's somewhat different from the one that's used in the function you're testing; otherwise, you incur the risk of having the same error in your check as in the function you're testing.

- **The 80/20 step-by-step guide.** I have prepared a step-by-step guide to automate 80% of your tasks with 20% of the efforts with MATLAB (first appendix). This can be a good place to start if you desperately need more time without having to invest too much efforts.

Appendix

Step-By-Step Guide to Automate 80% of Your Tasks With 20% of the Efforts With MATLAB

(Step 1) Identify your biggest, most strenuous, energy-intensive, and time-consuming tasks.

① What are the actions that you do most frequently (think several times a day)?

For example, do you have to open a file (e.g., Excel file, Word file) or a specific folder? It might be to document your progress on specific tasks. If you do, use **winopen** or **edit** in a shortcut or a quick access shortcut depending on the frequency. Do you have to move from folder to folder, rename files, or create a zip file out of several files frequently? If you do, use the **cd**, **movefile**, or **zip** commands.

② What are the most difficult tasks to do well systematically? Some tasks might need a lot of focus or you need to perform a set of tasks/verifications in a specific order (don't think about how to automate them for now, only identify them).

For example, when you're about to close a Simulink model you may want to double-check the library links, save your model, close it, clear your workspace, and re-open your model to run the simulation (see `https://realtechnologytools.com/matlab-model-based-design-1` to get the script to automate this). It's not a difficult task in and of itself but it's easy to either miss a step or make a mistake in the sequencing of the steps, thus it qualifies as a difficult set of tasks to do well systematically.

■ This step is essential because you need to **start from a relevant need,** if you use your time to automate a task of low added value to your work you'll end up with a very limited return on your time investment.

(Step 2) Write step-by-step procedures detailing every action performed during these tasks, then choose a procedure to focus on.

① Write down every click, every word you type, every folder you open, every file you rename, every text you copy and paste. Break everything down to a list of single steps.

② Based on these lists you can then roughly say which one is the longest or which one has the most complicated steps, i.e. better identify the procedure that best leverages your time once automated.

■ The simple act of writing these lists will clarify what you are actually doing when you perform one of these tasks and improve your productivity in and of itself. I recommend storing those procedures in an easy-to-access location so that you can use them when executing those tasks (I personally use an .org file). This step will enable you to **identify specific steps needed to execute your tasks,** i.e. potential candidates for automation.

(Step 3) Automate the relevant step(s), and switch to the next procedure.

(1) Identify the steps of the procedure from **(Step 2)** that are the easiest to automate relative to the benefits it would give you in terms of quality, time saved, frequency of use and energy saved.

(2) Automate these parts to the exclusion of the others. By excluding the other steps, you save 80% of your energy but you miss out on only 20% of the benefits of automation.

(3) Do the same for the next procedure you've identified using **(Step 1)** and **(Step 2)**.

■ This is the step where you **automate only the tasks that will make your life easier**, if automating one step of a task takes you so much time that you end up loosing time overall, then it's not worth automating.

Abbreviations

abbreviation	meaning
arg	argument
c	column
char	character
dbt	dialogBoxTitle
desc	description
dest	destination
dlg	dialog
elts	elements
ext	extension
f	fonction
fl	file

abbreviation	meaning
fdr	folder
ls	list
m	matrix
num	number
o	offset
out	output
p	path
pmt	prompt
r	row
sel	selection
sz	size
nm	name

1. The Basic Tools for Automation

Cells

description	command
define a cell	cell = {x}
access cell content	cell{:}
define a list	list = [{'firstWord'}; {'secondWord'}]
access a cell	list{i}
number of cells	numel(list)

Matrices

description	command
define matrix	m = [1 2; 3 4]
number of rows	size(m, 1)
number of columns	size(m, 2)
remove second column	m(:, 2) = □
remove second row	m(2, :) = □
inverse matrix	inv(m)
transpose of a matrix	m'
multiplying matrices	A*B
element by element	A.*B

Useful Functions

description	command
separate data	[token, remain] = strtok(variable, char)
split data	C = strsplit(variable, delimiter)
compare strings	strcmp(text1, text2)
number to string	num2str(numberToConvertToString)
string to number	str2num(stringToConvertToNumber)
check for content	isempty(variable)
compare lists	[newElts oldElts] = newOld(oldLs, newLs)

Standard Example:

strsplit
```
>> C = strsplit('w1 w2', ' ')
C =
  1x2 cell array
    'w1'  'w2'
```

strtok
```
>> [tkn, rmn] = strtok('fl.txt', '.')
tkn =
fl
rmn =
.txt
```

2. Extract and Generate Excel Files

description	command
read an Excel file	[num txt txtAndNum] = xlsread(flNm)
specify sheet name	xlsread(flNm, sheetName)
specify sheet number	xlsread(flNm, sheetNumber)
write an Excel file	xlswrite(flNm, data, sheetNumber)
store a matrix	storeMatrix(m, flNm, shtNm, p, o)

Standard Example:

read text in an Excel file
```
f1 = 'excelFile.xlsx';
sht = 1;
[-, txt, -] = xlsread(f1, sht)
```

write text in an Excel file
```
f1 = 'excelFile.xlsx';
sht = 1;
data = [{'firstWord'}; {'secondWord'}];
xlswrite(f1, data, sht);
```

3. Manipulate Files

Files and Folders

description	command
move a file	movefile(flNm, fullfile(dest, flNm))
copy a file	copyfile(flNm, fullfile(dest, flNm))
create a folder	mkdir(fdrNm)
delete a folder	rmdir(fdrNm, 's')
move a folder	movefile(fdrNm, fullfile(dest, fdrNm))
use the clock	c = clock % [year month day hour min]

Read Files in a Folder

description	command
list folder content	FilesAndFolders = dir
list .m files	files = dir('*.m')
list specific extension	files = dir(['*' extension])

Read and Write Files

description	command
open a file to write	fid = fopen('textFileName.txt', 'at')
open a file to read	fid = fopen('textFileName.txt')
write content	fprintf(fid, '%s\n', 'Text')
read a line	fgetl(fid)
close a file	fclose(fid)
replace words	strrep(textLine, oldText, newText)
check keyword	~isempty(strfind(textLine, keyword))
detect errors	assert(booleanValue, 'Error!')

Standard Example:

read a file
```
fid = fopen('flNm.txt');
while ~feof(fid)
    textline = fgetl(fid)
end
fclose(fid)
```

write a file
```
fid = fopen('flNm.txt', 'at');
fprintf(fid, '%s\n', "Text.');
fclose(fid);
```

Know If a File or a Folder Exists

Standard Example:

1 if it's a folder
```
if exist('folderName')==7
    ...
end
```

2 if it's a file
```
if exist('fileName.ext')==2
    ...
end
```

Generate LATEX Files

Standard Example:
```
fid = fopen('document.tex', 'at');
fprintf(fid, '%s', ['\documentclass[10pt]{article}' char(10)]);
fprintf(fid, '%s', ['\usepackage{mathpazo}' char(10) char(10)]);
fprintf(fid, '%s', ['%% comment' char(10)]);
fprintf(fid, '%s', ['\title{Generated Latex File}' char(10)]);
fprintf(fid, '%s', ['\begin{document}' char(10) char(10)]);

fprintf(fid, '%s', ['\maketitle' char(10)]);
fprintf(fid, '%s', ['\tableofcontents' char(10) char(10)]);
fprintf(fid, '%s', ['\section{Section}' char(10)]);
fprintf(fid, '%s', ['\begin{itemize}' char(10)]);
fprintf(fid, '%s', ['\item Bullet point' char(10)]);
fprintf(fid, '%s', ['\end{itemize}' char(10) char(10)]);

fprintf(fid, '%s', ['\end{document}' char(10)]);
fclose(fid);
```

Latex Functions

description	command
format matrix	fM = formatMatrixTex(matrix)
write a table	tableTex(fid, fM, h, colorH, forcedSz, fontSz)
fid	output of the fopen MATLAB function
fM	formatted matrix of cells
h	header of the matrix
colorH	color of the first line of the table
forcedSz	size of each column relative to full page width
fontSz	font size of the content of the table

4. User Interface

description	command
workspace query	inputArgument = input(prompt)
find a file	[flNm, pNm] = uigetfile(ext, dbt, fl)
use GUI	list = inputdlg(pmt, dlgTitle)

Special Characters

description	command
single quotation mark	char(39)
go to next line	char(10)
tabulation	char(9)

5. Best Practices on MATLAB: Improve Your Programming Skills

description	command
move location	cd(path)
add a path	addpath(path)
open in windows	winopen(file)
open in MATLAB editor	edit(file)
clean up	clear all; close all; bdclose all; clc
delete a file	delete('fileName.txt')

Use Structures

description	command
define a structure	structureNm.fieldNm = value
access an element	structNm.fieldNm
access struct array element	structNm(eltIndex).fieldNm
check for field	isfield(structureNm, fieldNm)
find field names	fieldnames(structureNm)
check for structure	isstruct(structureNm)

Define Shortcuts

1. make sure you are in the right location using cd(path)
2. add your path in the search path using addpath(path)
3. define your arguments
4. call your function

Backup Shortcuts

1. use winopen(prefdir)
2. save/backup shortcuts_2.xml
3. save/backup MATLABQuickAccess.xml

Keyboard Shortcuts

description	keyboard
run a script	F5
indent the selected code	CTRL+I
comment code	CTRL+R
uncomment code	CTRL+T
open corresponding .m file	CTRL+D
run a piece of code in a script	F9
stop the execution of a code	CTRL+C
jump between variables	ALT+UP/DOWN
open new script/close script	CTRL+N/CTRL+W
run a cell delimited by %%	CTRL+ENTER

Real Technology Tools, https://realtechnologytools.com

Understanding the Evalin Function and the Caller Workspace

The caller workspace is the workspace of the function "calling the one we are in" when we use the **evalin** function. For example:

```
1  function [out1, out2, ...] = functionA(arg1, arg2, ...)
2
3  valueOfTheString = functionB(string);
4
5  end
```

tools/functionA.m

The caller workspace of *functionB* is what you can access from *functionA*:

```
1  function valueOfTheString = functionB(string)
2
3  valueOfTheString = evalin('caller', string);
4
5  end
```

tools/functionB.m

In this example, the `string` will be executed as if it was an expression inside **functionA** and the result will be stored in the variable `valueOfTheString` in **functionB**.

What's the point? Sometimes, the name of a variable depends on some external factor, when that's the case, you have to find a way to change it. That's what we call "defining the name of a variable dynamically." From **functionB** you'll have access to the value of the variable `string` which means that you'll get to define the variable to be evaluated dynamically.

In other words:

- The idea behind using the **evalin** function is to define a variable based on the output of an expression (defined by the variable `string`).

- When we specify `'caller'` as the workspace, the evalin function "executes" the argument as a line of code, as if it was in **functionA** and returns the output in **functionB**.

- If the expression (i.e. the value of the variable `string`) is just the name of a variable, then you have to be able to access it from **functionA**.